# BOLD & BROKEN

## BROKEN

revisited

**SPEAKING TRUTH WITHOUT BACKING DOWN.
SHOWING LOVE WITHOUT LETTING GO.**

# BOLD & BROKEN

revisited

## SPEAKING TRUTH WITHOUT BACKING DOWN.
## SHOWING LOVE WITHOUT LETTING GO.

### DAVID AND JASON BENHAM

Entrepreneurs, Speakers, and Bestselling Authors of
*Whatever The Cost*

Bold And Broken (revisited):
*Speaking Truth Without Backing Down. Showing Love Without Letting Go.*

Learn more about the brothers at BenhamBrothers.com.

Published in Charlotte, North Carolina, by Benham Media.

Unless otherwise indicated, Scripture quotations are taken from the Holy Bible, New International Version* and New American Standard Bible*

…New International Version*, NIV*. © 1973, 1978, 1984, 2011 by Biblica, Inc.* Used by permission of Zondervan. All rights reserved worldwide.

…New American Standard Bible*, NASB*. © 1960, 1962, 1963, 1968, 1971, 1972, 1973, 1975, 1977, 1995 by The Lockman Foundation. Used by permission.

ISBN (paperback): 979-8-9923386-6-9

Printed in the United States of America

Bulk purchases available.
Contact through BenhamBrothers.com.

# DEDICATION

*To the Truth-Tellers of the world—those who refuse to bow to cultural pressure, who speak with courage when silence would be easier, and who carry compassion even when the world shows contempt. Your boldness shines light in dark places and builds bridges where others see only walls. This book is for you.*

# TABLE OF CONTENTS

# FOREWORD

*By Gabe Lyons*

W e're living in a cultural moment where those who dare to lead the conversation are putting themselves at risk. I said that recently to a room of 2,000 Christian leaders, and I meant every word. The cost of speaking truth in today's world is steep—but the cost of silence is far greater.

When I think about people who understand that tension—who live it, breathe it, and model it—my buddies David and Jason Benham come to mind.

Our friendship goes all the way back to the glory days at Liberty University in the mid-'90s—when baggy pants and tucked-in sweaters were peak fashion, and every weekend ended at Knowlesy's house for a dance party that probably broke a few Baptist rules. Afterward, we'd hit the Texas Inn for cheesy-western burgers, where our favorite waitress, Debbie, would greet us with sarcastic insults that somehow made us feel right at home.

Those were the nights we'd stay up too late debating theology, dreaming about the future, and, of course, analyzing the LU girl scene—usually in that order. Somewhere in all that chaos, a brotherhood was born that's lasted a lifetime.

I was honored to stand beside both brothers at their weddings and they at mine, and have been even more honored to walk beside them ever since. Through all the years, all the ventures, and all the battles, one thing has remained constant—they've never backed down from truth, and they've never lost their love for people. That's a rare combination.

The Benham brothers have taught me as much as I've ever taught them. Honestly, if I'm Luke Skywalker, they've been my Yodas—steady, grounded voices speaking truth when I needed it most. God has used their influence in my life in ways they probably don't even realize.

Over the years, God has used their steady influence to shape not just my life, but everything I lead. From my weekly men's Bible study to THINQ—the global media organization I founded—their conviction and steadfast commitment to grounding every idea in truth, no matter the cultural pressure, has strengthened my leadership and blessed all those I serve.

That's exactly why *Bold & Broken* is such an important book for this moment. It captures what our generation of believers needs most—the courage to stand for truth and the humility to stay surrendered to God while doing it. The Benhams don't write from theory; they write from the frontlines.

I'll never forget watching the guys get fired by HGTV back in 2014, when cancel culture decided their stand for biblical truth was too much to tolerate. Overnight, they became the number-one story on Facebook—literally across the world—as critics hurled insults and tried to shut them down. But they never flinched. They didn't retaliate or retreat; they spoke the truth with love, and they did it all with a smile on their face.

Watching that moment unfold left a permanent mark on me. Their courage to stand for truth, no matter the cost, inspired me to do the same. And I believe it will do the same for you.

We're living in a time when cultural currents are strong and the voices of truth are mocked, censored, or silenced. Far too many Christian leaders—including me, for a season—have stayed quiet when we should've spoken up. Fear of backlash, of losing influence, or of being misunderstood kept us from saying what needed to be said.

But that's changing. It has to.

The world doesn't need more polished silence—it needs courageous voices. Believers who will speak truth with conviction and compassion, even when it costs them something. That's what *Bold & Broken* is calling us back to—a faith that's fearless, grounded, and full of grace.

As you read this book, don't skim it. Soak it in. Let it stir your courage and reawaken your calling. Let it remind you that truth is still worth speaking and love is still worth showing, no matter the cost.

The world doesn't need louder Christians. It needs deeper ones. And this book will help you become exactly that.

— **Gabe Lyons**
Founder, THINQ Media

# AUTHOR'S NOTE

When we first released *Bold And Broken* in 2019, the world looked very different. Yes, there were challenges, but few of us could have imagined the tidal wave of social, cultural, and political unrest that would crash over the next six years.

A global pandemic brought the world to a halt, and with it came government-mandated shutdowns that forced churches to close their doors, isolated families in their homes, and reshaped daily life in ways we still feel today. Political violence has erupted like never before. Voices of dissent are being silenced and censored. And the mainstream media, once thought to be a watchdog for truth, has become a megaphone for lies—mocking, smearing, and bullying anyone who dares to stand for biblical values.

The clash between truth and lies has become bigger than ever. Ideas once whispered on the fringe are being shouted in the streets and codified into policy. We've seen families fracturing, churches splitting, and friendships ending over competing allegiances to ideologies instead of God's truth.

Then came the moment that elevated everything to a whole new height—the assassination of Charlie Kirk. His death wasn't just political; it was spiritual. And whether or not you agreed with him, it was the kind of moment that made the whole world stop, even for a second, and realize the battle we're in is not against flesh and blood, but against principalities and powers.

In the aftermath, several close friends told us, "Your Bold And Broken message is the message for this hour." That stirred us to revisit this book, not to rewrite it, but to take a fresh look at a timeless call.

Because this is the moment we were made for. Not a time for bullies who wield truth without love, or bystanders who feel compassion but shrink back in silence—but for bridges. People willing to stand in the gap, connecting heaven and earth with courage and compassion.

The world needs you. The time is now. We wrote this for you.

# INTRODUCTION

*"Courage is contagious.*
*When a brave man takes a stand,*
*the spines of others are stiffened."*
–Billy Graham

～

D o you remember where you were when the planes hit the Twin Towers on 9/11? If you were alive, you'll never forget. If you weren't, you've only known a post-9/11 world, because that day changed everything. It marked a turning point in our nation.

Life was never the same.

For a brief moment, America woke up. We dropped the labels—Republican, Democrat, conservative, liberal, rich, poor. We weren't enemies anymore. We were brothers and sisters, united against a common threat. What made that possible? Not a new program, not a bestselling book, not even a shared faith. It was the call of battle. We suddenly realized we weren't fighting each other—we were fighting together against a real enemy who wanted us destroyed.

That was the wake-up call of 9/11.

Two dozen years later, we were shaken again. On 9/10, when Charlie Kirk was assassinated, people around the world felt the ground shift. His death marked another turning point—not just for a nation, but for the Church.

If 9/11 opened our eyes to a physical battle, 9/10 opened our eyes to a spiritual one.

For the two of us, we had just wrapped up a two-day mastermind meeting with a group of entrepreneurs, riding the high of breakthrough moments and big visions for the future. Then suddenly, everything shifted.

At first, we were confused. Our phones started buzzing, and social media was blowing up with wild headlines. Was it real? Was it another AI deepfake? We didn't know what to believe. But then the videos started rolling in. Grainy at first, then crystal clear. And the horrible truth sank in.

Charlie Kirk had been shot and killed.

Without hesitation, we scrolled, desperate for clarity. And what we found horrified us. Clip after clip, angle after angle—Charlie's public assassination replayed across our screens, followed by chaos, screaming, and panic. It felt surreal, like a nightmare you can't wake up from.

No words can fully capture what that moment did to us. Here was a young man, standing on a university campus, doing what he always did—engaging in open dialogue with students, talking about faith, culture, and truth. He did what others wouldn't do—allow his ideas to be challenged by all takers, in public, for all to hear. He wasn't hiding behind a keyboard or retreating when things got heated. He showed up. He had the courage to stand in the gap. And for that, he was gunned down.

I (Jason) remember my whole body going numb at the sight of Charlie getting hit and falling off his chair. My chest tightened as my mind started racing. Shock gave way to sorrow, and sorrow to anger. I couldn't believe what I was seeing. A man murdered, not for committing a crime but for having the courage to speak what he believed.

At that moment, I knew this was bigger than politics, bigger than opinions. I was staring at the cost of conviction. And it rocked me to my core.

For a few brief moments, we thought he might make it. Someone said he still had a pulse. But then I saw it unfold live. Megan Kelly was on air with Glenn Beck when the confirmation came. Megan's voice cracked as she delivered the words, fighting back tears. Glenn couldn't hold his composure—he broke down in sobs. Two influential voices, completely undone by the death of a 31-year-old husband and father.

They weren't alone. Across the globe, grief hit like a tidal wave. Celebrities, commentators, pastors, ordinary people—so many who had never even met Charlie—mourned as if they'd lost a brother or a son. His death cut deep, crossing lines of politics, nationality, and even religion. For a brief moment, the world stopped and grieved together. (Well, *most* of the world— we'll get into that later).

Crowds filled the streets with chants of *"We are Charlie."* But what stunned us most wasn't just the global response—it was the fire his death lit within the Church. Young believers everywhere began declaring they wanted to go all-in for their faith, no more half measures, no more compromises.

But with that fire also came fury.

In the days that followed, we saw countless posts and videos filled with anger, outrage, and threats. People wanted vengeance. They wanted to strike back. And on one level, we understood it—when someone you admire is taken from you in such a brutal way, it's natural to want vengeance. But anger alone can be dangerous—because *boldness apart from brokenness makes a bully*. And bullies don't build bridges; they burn them.

I (David) remember scrolling social media and seeing radical leftists—talk show hosts, professors, influencers—condemning Charlie's "divisive" words, some even seeming to excuse his murder. I was stunned. Then I felt a fire in my chest—righteous indignation. But I also knew if I wasn't careful, that fire could blaze into unrighteous condemnation.

This was a moment to engage—but to engage *faithfully*. That balance felt impossible in the heat of the moment. Yet one thing was clear: if we let anger drive us, we'd miss the point of Charlie's life. He wasn't killed because he hated—he was killed because he loved enough to tell the truth.

Charlie wasn't perfect by any stretch. If he were alive today, he'd probably admit to plenty of regrets. But here's what set him apart: he did what his critics always claimed to want. He engaged in honest conversations and open dialogue. And he didn't do it in secret; he did it out in the open, where anyone could challenge him. That takes guts. Most of us would shrink back. Charlie stepped forward.

And in doing so, he became more than a voice. He became a bridge—linking a broken world to an unshakable God.

The day after Charlie's death, we knew people were searching for how to respond—how to make sense of the moment without being swallowed by fear or rage. So we posted a message on social media, pointing to two defining moments in Peter's life that show us exactly what we need to see today.

The first moment came when Jesus told His disciples that He was going to Jerusalem to die. Peter, full of good intentions, jumped in:

*"This shall never happen to you!"* (Matthew 16:22).

How did Jesus respond?

*"Get behind me, Satan!"* (Matthew 16:23).

Jesus wasn't calling Peter *Satan*—He was exposing the dark spirit behind Peter's words. Peter's intentions may have been good, but his perspective was influenced by the enemy. That's the warning for us today: good intentions don't always mean godly influence. We must keep our eyes wide open to discern the spirit behind the message—our own and that of others.

The second moment came in the Garden of Gethsemane. Soldiers arrived to arrest Jesus, but Peter wasn't having it. He pulled out his sword, swung for a soldier's head, and clipped off his ear instead.

How did Jesus respond?

*"Put your sword back in its place"* (Matthew 26:52).

Once again, Jesus had to remind Peter—this was not a physical fight but a spiritual one. And in a spiritual battle, God's people are not called to hurt but to heal, not to destroy but to redeem. At a time like this, courage is never an excuse for cruelty. Boldness for truth must always be anchored in the compassion of Christ.

Watching it all unfold that day, we knew immediately: this was more than politics. This was a spiritual war. Not just a political assassination—a spiritual confrontation.

Charlie stood toe to toe with the darkness as he carried the blazing light of God's Word. He had a rare gift—to take timeless Scripture and make it clear, simple, and practical for the next generation.

And that is why he was targeted. Not for hate. Not for violence. But because he dared to fight on the most dangerous battlefield of all—the battlefield of ideas.

God loves all people, but He does not love all ideas. Some ideas are toxic. Some destroy lives. And Scripture tells us exactly what to do with them:

*"We demolish arguments and every pretension that sets itself up against the knowledge of God"* (2 Corinthians 10:5).

This is where Charlie fought. Not with fists, not with swords—but in the arena of ideas. And this is where we need to fight, too.

But here's the warning: if we charge into this battle with only boldness, our words become weapons that wound instead of heal. We turn into bullies. And if we shrink back with only brokenness, grieving the state of the world but never speaking up, we fade into bystanders. In the flesh, we naturally tend toward one or the other.

But there's a better way—Boldness anchored in brokenness. Truth spoken with tears. Conviction carried with compassion. That's what makes you a bridge between heaven and earth.

Charlie's life modeled this type of boldness. Was he perfect? No. None of us are. We may not have agreed with everything he said—especially in his younger years. But he was a powerful testimony of Christian courage—and for that, we honor him. His willingness to face hatred, endure ridicule, and pay the ultimate price marks him as a man who stood in the gap.

Now the mantle has fallen on our shoulders. We can't afford to retreat into silence or lash out in rage.

We can't drift into the ditch of boldness without love, becoming bullies.

But neither can we collapse into the ditch of brokenness without courage, becoming bystanders.

We are called to rise and fill the gap as bridges—humble warriors who combine tenderness with tenacity.

This is our 9/10 turning point. This is where we decide if we'll waste Charlie's sacrifice, or if we'll pick up the torch and stand in the gap ourselves. The world doesn't need more bullies or bystanders. The world needs bridges.

And make no mistake, God is still searching, just as He was in Ezekiel's day:

*"I looked for someone among them who would build up the wall and stand before me in the gap"* (Ezekiel 22:30).

The need has never been greater. The battle has never been clearer. The call has never been louder.

In the pages ahead, we'll show you what it means to stand in the gap—to become a bridge between heaven and earth in real, practical ways. You'll hear our stories, and the stories of ordinary men and women who stepped into that sacred calling.

The time is now. The gap is wide. God is calling you. Will you stand?

We believe you will. It won't be easy, but it will be worth it. So grab your coffee (or protein shake) and join us—we'll start with a story that takes us to a Chicago Cubs baseball game.

# CHAPTER ONE
# CHICAGO

*"True compassion means not only
feeling another's pain but also being
moved to help relieve it."*
–Daniel Goleman

~

I f you know anything about our story, you might remember
that in May of 2014, our HGTV reality show was abruptly
canceled due to activist groups pressuring the network to pull
the plug. Why? Because we had been vocal about our faith in the
public square, sharing God's truth on issues many considered
"politically incorrect." The backlash was fierce. Overnight, we
were smeared across the internet, called every name imaginable.
This was cancel culture before before it became a popular
hashtag.

We'll unpack more of this in chapter four, but a few
days after our show was canceled, and while our faces were
still plastered all over social media, we got a private message
on Facebook from a man in Chicago. By that point, the clash
between our stand for biblical values and the culture's outrage
had reached a fever pitch, and it wasn't exactly bringing out the
best in people. This man was no exception. Angry doesn't even
begin to describe his DM—he was absolutely furious.

The venom this man was spewing as he ripped into us turned our stomachs upside down. Initially, we both felt the knee-jerk reaction to boldly defend and debate. We grew up fighters, so we have no problem locking horns. And as twins, fighting is in our DNA.

## Yeah, We Fight a Little

We were raised by a pastor dad in Dallas, TX. He trained us to be fighters, in every sense of the term. When we were kids, he loved to watch us box. For Christmas each year, we'd buy each other Sugar Ray Leonard boxing gloves. We'd pull them from under the tree and, like clockwork, we'd start wailing on each other while Dad shadow-boxed the air as he watched us.

We'd hear Mom in the background, "Flip, stop them! They're being too rough."

"Nah, this is good for them," he'd tell her as he threw a phantom left jab while holding his right hand by his face. "They need to learn how to defend themselves."

I (Jason) guess now would be a good time to tell you David's defense was never as good as mine. When we were fourteen years old, I dropped him in a backyard boxing match with a lightning-fast jab to the chin. When he regained consciousness, he started screaming, "All I see is green!" It was the most amazing feeling a boy could ever have. My eyes still well up with tears of joy thinking about that moment.

That same fighter's instinct rose up in us when we got the message from the man in Chicago. *We've got to defend ourselves,* we thought, and we were ready to pounce and set the record straight. By then our reputations were already dragged through the mud, smeared with lies and accusations. So, our gut reaction was to slip back into those old backyard brawls—only this time, the fight would be with words.

Of course, at that moment we weren't thinking of Christ's words:

*"Blessed are you when people insult you, persecute you and falsely say all kinds of evil about you because of me"* (Matthew 5:11).

Within seconds, the Holy Spirit checked our boldness and reminded us of brokenness, bringing that beautiful balance only the Spirit can bring. Our hearts broke for this man because we were reminded of our own past sin issues and how merciful God has always been with us.

At that moment we didn't need to win our point; we needed to win a person. This man's argument against us did not represent a fight to win but a person to love. And we couldn't do this without first walking in brokenness.

So, we responded, "We see you're upset at us, but what we know is that you're simply speaking through your pain."

He must have been on Facebook at the same time because within minutes he shot back what seemed like the longest response in Facebook Messenger history. He basically dumped his life story on us, and with every word we read, our hearts grieved even more for him. He was trying to find the love of a father in the arms of another man.

He was a man who was disconnected from the God who created him, loved him, and had a wonderful plan for him. He had a daddy-gap that could be filled only by his Heavenly Father. God caused our paths to cross so we could be a part of standing in that gap.

With hearts full of compassion for this man, we engaged in conversation, telling him how God had radically transformed our own lives because He loves us and wants what's best for us, and He could do the same for him. We then explained how God loves him just like he is but refuses to leave him that way—because He's too good a God to leave us like we are, captured by our sin.

We've got to be honest here. Telling him that last part—God had something better for him than his current lifestyle—was not easy. When our hearts broke for him, we didn't want to hurt his feelings in any way or turn him off. But we also knew God had the answer to his current situation, and he needed to hear it. We were already convicted of being bold bullies, but now we were tempted to be broken bystanders. (Telling the truth in love isn't easy.) Fortunately, the Holy Spirit working in us was able to bring the balance.

Interestingly, in the course of the conversation, we discovered this guy was an avid Chicago Cubs fan. Prompted by the Lord, we told him we wanted to get two front row tickets for him and a friend to a Cubs game at Wrigley Field.

There's simply nothing like smashing a ballpark dog on game day at Wrigley when the Cardinals are in town. Seriously, if you haven't done it, put that on your bucket list.

The man was gracious in his response, thanking us for being willing to buy him tickets, but he refused. We pressed, "Come on man—let us send you and a friend to the game. You'll love it!"

What he said next ripped our hearts out. "I don't have any friends."

Can you imagine how difficult it must have been for him to write those five words? It's even hard to write this now without feeling deep emotion for him. Here's a man who was once a boy with a mom who loved him, friends who liked him, and hopes and dreams of what he wanted to be one day. Now, he was just a broken man void of hope and the deep relationships none of us can survive without.

We pressed in a bit more, and he finally agreed to go to the game, alone.

A few days later, he sent us a message with these words: "Thank you so much for what you did. I've been listening to this song [he sent a link to Mercy Me's song, *I Can Only Imagine*], and I've decided to leave my lifestyle and turn back to God."

What?! It's never that simple. But God had been working on this guy's heart all along, narrowing the gap between heaven and earth in his heart. All he needed was a little more love, and God used Cubs tickets and a Mercy Me song to seal the deal! It was amazing to be a part of God's work in this man's life.

This guy's story is just one small example of the gaps in our culture—gaping holes created by the demonic forces of this world that seek to maintain control over the people God created in His image. You probably know people just like him right now—people who need a bridge back to their Creator so they can taste the abundant life only He gives.

The question is, will you be that bridge, even when it's hard?

Are you willing to step up to this calling?

That day with our Chicago friend wasn't just a passing moment—it was a divine assignment. And it's the same assignment we carry every single day: to stand in the gap, to be bridges between heaven and earth, connecting God with those far from Him, even when it's uncomfortable.

Truth without love can crush, and love without truth can mislead, but together they open a path for people to encounter God.

Every conversation, every act of courage, every step of compassion is part of the greater clash between the Kingdom of Light and the kingdom of darkness. And when you step into that calling—when you choose to be Bold And Broken—you step onto the winning side.

This is the fight we were made for. And in the next chapter, we'll pull back the curtain to show you what this fight really looks like—the Kingdom Collision at the heart of it all.

## CHAPTER TWO

# A KINGDOM COLLISION

*"The moment of impact proves potential for change.
It has ripple effects far beyond what we can predict …
You just gotta let the colliding parts go where they may.
And wait for the next collision."*
—Leo in *The Vow*

Everywhere we look, the battle is raging. It's not just politics, culture wars, or social unrest; it's the clash of kingdoms. Light against darkness. Truth against lies. Heaven against hell. And whether we realize it or not, every one of us is caught in the middle of this fight. The battle is real, and the stakes couldn't be higher.

If we're going to step into this war the way God intends, we can't do it half-heartedly. It takes boldness to stand for truth when the world mocks you, and it takes brokenness to carry God's heart for people who oppose you. Put the two together, and your life becomes a bridge that heaven can walk across to touch earth. That's what real Kingdom impact looks like. But before we can live it, we need to define it.

Voltaire once said, "If you want to converse with me, first define your terms."[1]

Satan is good at redefining words. That's how he takes over a culture. We see this happening before our eyes today, so we want to clarify our words right out of the gate.

As believers, we use the word *kingdom* a lot. We talk about "building the Kingdom," "advancing the Kingdom," or "living for the Kingdom." But if we don't stop to define what that means, it just becomes another churchy word we toss around without much weight. And when words lose their meaning, they lose their power.

The same is true with the word *impact*. Everyone wants their life to matter. We want to leave a mark, to make a difference. But true impact isn't about fame, followers, or influence; it's about standing in the gap so that heaven touches earth through us. And to understand how to live that kind of life, we first need to define these two important words.

Let's start with the word "kingdom." It comes from two root words: "king" and "dominion." A kingdom is a realm defined by the rule or dominion of a king.

The next question is: which king?

The answer is simple—Jesus.

It's not about King George, King Henry, Caesar, Pharaoh, or any other earthly ruler. It's solely about King Jesus and His reign.

For believers, the Kingdom refers to the Kingdom of God, and is centered on Jesus and His rightful rule. He is meant to govern every aspect of our lives—our hearts, cities, nations, and, ultimately, the world. Jesus is a good king. He never forces anyone to submit to His authority; it is always a voluntary act of love and surrender.

At present, Jesus rules spiritually. But one day, when He returns, He will rule physically and visibly over all creation.

Jesus governs according to His Word—the Bible—which clearly outlines what the King expects from His people. This is why daily study of Scripture is so essential. It's not just a religious practice; it's the foundation for understanding and living under His rule. We can confidently say that the best decisions we've ever made—whether in building businesses, raising families, managing money, or making an impact—have come from consistent prayer and Bible reading. There is nothing—absolutely nothing—that surpasses the power of those two habits.

Dr. Tony Evans defines the "Kingdom of God" as *the comprehensive rule of God in every area of life.*[2]

This encompasses everything—your marriage, how you raise your kids, the policies and operations of government, the stewardship of your financial resources, how you run your business, and even how you engage with your community and culture. It includes your relationships, your work ethic, and how you use your time.

Nothing is outside the scope of God's rule. Every aspect of life, from the smallest details to the most significant global systems, is meant to align under His authority and reflect His Kingdom.

Psalm 24:1 reminds us, "*The earth is the Lord's and everything in it.*"

Imagine taking a sheet of paper and drawing a line down the middle. On the right side, you list everything God cares about and has an answer for. On the left side, you list everything He doesn't care about or have an answer for. What would you find on the left side? Absolutely nothing! God cares about everything and has a solution for it all.

As believers, this means we should be willing to engage with all areas of life. We are called to live in alignment with His Kingdom, and when we do, we actively fulfill the prayer of Christ:

"... *Thy kingdom come, Thy will be done on earth as it is in heaven*" (Matthew 6:9-13).

How does God bring heaven to earth today? Through His people. He accomplished the initial work of breaking down the walls of partition through His Son, and now He continues His work through the Church—that's us. His Kingdom has already come *down* from heaven through the person of Jesus. Now, it's our responsibility to get the Kingdom *out* of us and into the world.

When we live like this—honoring King Jesus and speaking the truth—we will have an impact.

## Brace For Impact

Now, let's take a moment to define the word impact.

Impact is *the collision of two opposing forces.*[3]

Here's the critical point: There exists another kingdom on earth that stands in opposition to the Kingdom of Heaven. It is known as the Kingdom of Darkness, ruled by Satan. We will explain in the next chapter how he came to rule that kingdom.

For now, understand this: When we live our lives with Christ as our King, we will inevitably collide with Satan's kingdom.

It's not that we *might* collide with Satan; we *will* collide with him. The Kingdom of Darkness utterly despises the Kingdom of Light. The forces of Hell are in direct opposition to the Kingdom of Heaven. As a result, they relentlessly wage war against it.

This war takes many forms. It appears as a hit piece in the local paper, attacking a Christian business owner for supporting a faith-based charity. It surfaces when a devoted leader speaks out against a city ordinance aimed at silencing pro-life sidewalk counselors. It shows itself when a generous philanthropist supports a Christian candidate who stands against the worldview promoted by mainstream media. You see it when a group of moms organize to stop the indoctrination of perversity that's taking place in grade schools all over the country; or, tragically, when a young 31-year-old Charlie Kirk is silenced for speaking truth on a college campus.

The Kingdom of Darkness will never sit by quietly and allow the Kingdom of Light to prevail. It is constantly at war, aggressively pushing back and exerting its force against those who dare to stand up and say "Jesus is King" over all creation, including the hot-button issues.

But here's the good news: As believers, we don't fight *for* victory—we fight *from* it. Jesus assured us that the gates of hell will not prevail against the Church (God's people fully submitted to His rule).

## Colliding And Overcoming

Now that we understand the meaning of the Kingdom—the rule of God over every area of life—and that impact is the collision of two opposing forces, let's see what happens when we bring these two words together:

Kingdom Impact is the *Kingdom of Heaven colliding with and overcoming the Kingdom of Hell.*

It's not just a collision; it's an overcoming. Our role as believers is not to shrink back and avoid the collision; our role is to surge forward and overcome it.

If you avoid the collision, you forfeit the impact.

You can avoid it if you want; that's the safe route. Many churches have taken that route, backing away from conversations that desperately need truth. In doing so, they strip the warning label off the Bible and replace it with a party invitation, turning the church from a boot camp into a bounce house, making it no longer a threat to the enemy.

Satan is okay with a church just sitting there and growing (or even better for him, stagnating) because it poses no threat. He's cool with people backing out of the fight for truth in the public square and choosing to play it safe rather than risk their lives and reputations to speak it boldly. But God has called us for impact, which means there will be a collision.

## This Little Light Of Mine

The problem today is not the presence of darkness—it's the absence of light! Think about it: do you have any "dark switches" in your house that turn the darkness on? Of course not! You have "light switches" that turn the light on.

When you open a closet door, does the darkness from inside the closet spill out into the room? No! The light from the room floods into the closet, driving out the darkness.

This is because darkness isn't a force or "thing" on its own— it's simply the absence of a thing. And that thing is light! If the light doesn't shine, darkness takes over. That's why Scripture repeatedly calls us to be the "Light of the world."

Our mission is clear as believers: we are called to shine our light boldly. And when we do, we should expect to collide with the darkness. But that's precisely how the light overcomes it.

Today, many of us have a skewed understanding of what it means to be the light. Growing up in the '80s, we attended Sunday School before church every week, and without fail, we'd sing the classic song *This Little Light of Mine*. Do you remember that one?

There's a verse that goes, "This little light of mine, I'm gonna let it shine... Don't let Satan blow it out..." It's catchy and fun, but as we've grown older, we've come to understand that the idea of Satan being able to "blow" our light out distorts the image of the kind of light we should be.

When we sing that song, the image that comes to mind is a candle. A famous '90s song even told us to "*carry your candle into the darkness.*" But what happens to the light of a candle when the wind blows on it? It goes out!

Today, we need to replace the image of a *candle* with that of a *coal*—like the burning ember inside a fire pit. What happens when the wind blows on it? It ignites!

Do you see the difference? The same wind that *extinguishes* the candle's light *ignites* the coal.

What's the difference between a candle and a coal? A candle is lit from the outside. A coal burns from the inside.

The great prophet Jeremiah said, "*Your word is like a fire shut up in my bones, and I am weary of holding it in*" (Jeremiah 20:9).

Do you know how God gets the light that's in you out into the world? He often puts you in situations—and even around people—who will try to extinguish that light. But if you've been spending time with Him daily, nurturing the flame of His love in your heart through prayer and Bible study, these attempts to blow out your light will only serve to ignite it even brighter!

You don't have to *try* to shine your light at that moment— you just have to buckle up and let yourself burn.

When you shine your light, there will be impact—a head-on collision between the light in you and the darkness in the world.

But here's the good news: light always wins. Darkness doesn't stand a chance. That's a promise guaranteed since the very beginning of time.

## CHAPTER THREE

# IN THE BEGINNING

*"The beginning is the most
important part of the work."*
–Plato

~

So, where did all this begin—this idea of collision? Well, let us ask you this: what was the first sin? It's a bit of a trick question. If you said Adam and Eve in your mind, that was our first thought, too. However, the first sin actually took place before Adam and Eve; it occurred in heaven when Satan desired God's throne.

Satan was once an angel in heaven named Lucifer. But pride crept into his heart, and he wanted his own kingdom, his own throne. In an act of ultimate rebellion, he dared to challenge God Himself for supremacy.

Revelation 12 tells the story of this challenge. God didn't fight Lucifer Himself—that wouldn't have been a fair fight. Instead, He instructed the Archangel Michael to do the job. Let's dive into the story:

*"Then war broke out in heaven. Michael and his angels fought against the dragon, and the dragon and his angels fought back"* (Revelation 12:7).

How did this massive angelic battle turn out?

"*The great dragon was thrown down, that ancient serpent called the devil or Satan, who leads the whole world astray*" (Revelation 12:9a).

Satan … got … smacked! He and his angels (turned demons) got their rumps beat to a pulp.

What did God do with them?

"*… he was thrown down to the earth, and his angels were thrown down with him*" (Revelation 12:9b).

Where did God send Satan and the demons? Earth!

Let us ask you this: If you were God, and you created the angels with a spoken word, and then a large group of them rebelled against you, wanting to take your throne, how would you handle it? You probably would've simply spoken a word, snapped your fingers, and they would be gone. At least, that's what we would've done.

But God didn't do that in heaven. He *defeated* Satan, yet He didn't *destroy* him. That destruction is reserved for a future time. In the meantime, where is Satan?

He's here, on Earth.

And where are the demons?

In the exact same place—on Earth.

Did you know this battle described in Revelation 12 sets the stage for the entire Bible? You can't fully understand the

Book of Genesis without grasping what happened in Revelation 12.

The opening of the Bible states, "*In the beginning, God created the heavens and the earth*" (Genesis 1:1).

The very next verse tells us who was present:

"*Now the earth was formless and void, and darkness was over the surface of the deep*" (Genesis 1:2).

Darkness was present, which means that before the Earth was shaped into the ball we know today—with land, oceans, plants, animals, and everything else—Satan was already there.

No sooner did Satan find himself on the earth, away from God's presence, than God burst onto the scene:

"*Let there be LIGHT!*" (Genesis 1:3).

Genesis 1 is not simply about creation; it's about a *collision*—the Kingdom of Light colliding with and overcoming the Kingdom of Darkness!

I'm sure Satan didn't appreciate that very much, but impact always involves a collision. The Kingdom of Light confronts the Kingdom of Darkness, and when it does, it always wins.

Darkness only exists when light is turned off. As believers, our job is to turn the light on in the places of darkness, just as God did at the beginning of creation. And when we do, we can expect Satan to react, just as he did in the garden, as you'll soon see.

Back to Genesis 1. After Light entered the mix, what else did God do? He created. And on the sixth day, He reached the pinnacle of His work:

"*Then God said, 'Let us make man in our image, after our likeness ...'*" (Genesis 1:26).

God wasn't finished with Satan by simply casting him down to the earth. He was about to address the rebellion once and for all. But how would He do it?

He created another being—one unlike the angels—handcrafted in His own image. God created mankind, making them "*male and female*" (Genesis 5:2).

Hold up—we can't just breeze past what's happening here. This is huge, and it deserves some real thought. Let's take a moment to dig into the key aspects of mankind's creation. There are three big things we need to look at:

- Where God placed them.
- How He made them.
- What He gave them.

Each is packed with meaning, so let's give them the attention they deserve.

Beginning with where God placed them ...

On Earth—the very same place where He had just cast His arch-enemy, Satan, along with his hooligan demons.

Can you imagine that? God took His cherished, innocent image-bearers and placed them in the very location where He had just confined Satan.

Would you do that with your children—put them in a place where you knew someone wanted to harm them? Not a chance! But that is precisely what God did with us (you'll see why shortly).

Second, how did God make them?

Mankind was made "*a little lower than the angels*" (Psalms 8:5). This means we carry aspects of God's nature within us, but we're not as strong or powerful as angels. Why would God create beings like Himself but weaker than the angelic ones He had already made?

We believe it's because God wanted to demonstrate what He could accomplish with the "lesser" when the lesser was fully devoted to Him—far more than He could do with the greater when the greater was not devoted to Him.[4]

We know that's a mouthful, but read it again. Satan and the fallen angels, although more powerful than humans, could never match the strength of humanity when humanity is wholly surrendered to God. Earth became the proving ground for this reality.

You see, God didn't simply defeat Satan in Heaven— He humiliates him with "lesser beings" before He ultimately destroys him at the end.

This is why Psalm 110:1 is the most quoted Old Testament verse in the New Testament: "*The Lord says to my Lord: Sit at my right hand until I make your enemies a footstool under your feet.*"

The image here shows a victorious Jesus seated on His throne beside the Father. His feet rest on the ground as He waits—for what? For Satan to be made a *footstool* for His feet.

Picture this: Satan, on all fours, crawling to where Jesus is seated; and Jesus picking His feet up and resting them on his back. That's humiliation on a cosmic scale.

Here's an analogy to bring this idea home: Imagine you challenge me (Jason) to a fight, and I win. That would sting, no doubt. But imagine if, instead of fighting you myself, I said my 8-year-old daughter would handle it. Then, my little image-bearer, who shares some of my traits, wipes the floor with you. How would you feel then? You wouldn't just be defeated—you'd be *humiliated*!

Psalm 110:1 is repeated throughout the New Testament as a reminder of God's ultimate plan—to not only defeat Satan but to humiliate him completely before his final destruction.

As God's image-bearers, fully devoted to our King, we have a part to play in this. We're in the *footstool-making* business. Our role is to show Satan how much more God can do with the "lesser" (that's us) when we are devoted to Him than He can do with the "greater" (that's Satan) when the greater is not devoted to Him.

Mind blowing!

Now, let's dive into the third aspect of mankind's creation: What did God give them?

"... *And let them have dominion over the fish of the sea and over the birds of the heavens and over the livestock and over all the earth and over every creeping thing that creeps on the earth*" (Genesis 1:26).

*Dominion*—He gave them authority over everything. The very thing Satan desired in heaven, God now granted to Adam and Eve on Earth.

What do you think Satan wanted?

Authority.

Pause for a moment. Authority and responsibility are linked. The key to maintaining your authority is to stay in your place of responsibility. Satan cannot steal your authority—you have to give it to him. How? By failing in your responsibility.

God knew that Satan would attempt to seize mankind's authority, yet we have no scripture indicating that God warned Adam or Eve that he would come for it. All we know is that God gave them a job to do and a boundary to obey.

Adam's job was to cultivate—that is, to work for a reward (more on this in chapter four). Their boundary was simple: not to eat the fruit from one particular tree.

Isn't it interesting that boundaries existed before sin entered the world? God's blessings are always found within His boundaries.

But we all know how the story unfolds: Satan convinced Eve to cross that boundary and eat the fruit while her hubby sat quietly by—not protesting, not speaking up—just sitting in dead silence (sounds like some pastors today). He failed in his responsibility, and at that moment, he surrendered his authority to Satan. From that point forward in scripture, Satan is acknowledged as the "*ruler of this world*" (John 14:30).

All because of Adam's silence.

Famous Hebrew scholar Skip Moen said of this, "Adam knows what God commanded, but he does not oppose, remind, confront, exhort, or in any other way attempt to dissuade the woman from her intended act. His silent partnership leads directly to communal disaster."

Adam's silence = Satan's kingdom.

But the story doesn't end with Adam's failure; it only sets the stage for a greater victory. God sent His Son, Jesus, to Earth, and in the New Testament, Christ is called the "Second Adam." The Second Adam came to fix up what the first Adam messed up. He lived a sinless life, died a brutal death, and took back the authority Satan had stolen.

And here's the game-changer: Jesus didn't just reclaim that authority—He now gives it to *those who believe!* That's right. You and I represent the Kingdom of Light in this epic clash with the Kingdom of Darkness.

We're not just spectators in this battle. We are called to be God's ambassadors, His chosen representatives. And what do ambassadors do? They rule in the place of a king wherever they go.

That's our mission—to glorify God and represent His Kingdom on Earth. Every time we live out that calling, we push Satan closer to his destiny as a footstool under Christ's feet, keeping him firmly in his defeated state until the day he's ultimately destroyed.

This isn't just good news—it's life-altering, world-shaking news! But make no mistake: when you choose to live this way, you paint a target on your back. We know, because we found that out the hard way.

## CHAPTER FOUR

# HERE COMES THE BOOM

*"Persecution is one of the natural consequences of living the Christian life. It is to the Christian what 'growing pains' are to the growing child. No pain, no development. No suffering, no glory. No struggle, no victory. No persecution, no reward!"*
–Billy Graham

In chapter two, we explored our responsibility to be the light of the world and the inevitable collision with darkness that comes with it. But when you live as a bridge, you can expect resistance. Darkness doesn't sit quietly while light advances.

Now, in this chapter, we'll share our story—a real-life glimpse into what happens when you use your voice and resources to make an impact in your city. What we quickly realized is that the forces of darkness aren't passive observers; they push back, and they push hard.

When you shine your light in the world, the response will vary—some people will welcome it while others will reject it. It's like the effect of boiling water: it softens the carrot but hardens the egg. The same light that draws some people closer will cause others to turn away.

In Matthew 5:16, Jesus reminds us, "*Let your light so shine before men, that they may see your good works, and glorify your Father in heaven.*"

However, in John 3:20, He also warns us: "*Everyone who does evil hates the light, and will not come into the light for fear that their deeds will be exposed.*"

Some may love you, and some may hate you.

This dynamic illustrates the scriptural concept of a "balancing truth." It's not always one way or the other. As we let our light shine, we must be prepared for acceptance and resistance—they are both part of the calling.

Here's a balancing truth we've learned: While faithfulness in your *work* can lead to promotion, faithfulness in your *walk* can lead to persecution.

Proverbs 22:29 says, "*Do you see a man skilled in his work? He will stand before KINGS. He will not stand before obscure men.*" (emphasis added)

The man who's good at what he does, who is he going to stand in front of? *Kings!* In modern-day language, this means that when you're good at what you do in your work, you move up the ladder.

The balancing truth is found in the words of Jesus in Luke 21:12: "*But before all this, they will seize you and persecute you. They will hand you over to synagogues and put you in prison, and you will be brought before KINGS and governors, and all on account of My name.*" (emphasis added)

The one who's faithful to follow Christ, who will he stand in front of? *Kings!* In modern-day language, following Jesus and standing for His truth will fly in the face of culture and often get you in trouble.

We call this the "reward dichotomy." Faithfulness in your *work* puts you before kings on the one hand. But faithfulness in your *walk* puts you before kings on the other.

The same faithfulness that leads to promotion in one scenario can easily lead to persecution in another.

This is exactly what happened to Peter when he preached a message of repentance after Jesus ascended into heaven. Take a look at the responses of two different crowds to the same message he delivered:

"*So those who received his word were baptized, and there were added that day about three thousand souls*" (Acts 2:41).

"*When they heard this, they were enraged and wanted to kill them*" (Acts 5:33).

For Peter, it was promotion from the one crowd—3k people got saved—but persecution from the other. They wanted to kill him. Yet he preached the exact same message to both crowds.

Our job isn't to chase promotion or avoid persecution but to remain faithful. God determines which path we'll walk.

Back to our story. After more than a decade of enjoying God's favor and promotion in business, we were about to get our first real taste of persecution.

## Reality Check

We started our first business in 2003 with no formal business training. But we made a promise to God: we would read the Bible cover to cover each year and apply what we learned to our business and investments.

That simple plan became the foundation of everything. By 2010, we had grown that company into 100 offices across 35 states. At the same time, we lived by the "Proverbs 27" principle regarding income—living below our means and aggressively investing the rest. By God's grace, we reached 100% financial freedom by our mid-thirties.

We could have retired then and there, but the more we prayed, the clearer it became: God didn't give us income just to sit back and relax—He gave it to us for impact. So, instead of slowing down, we hit the gas. We launched new companies in different industries while continuing to live as frugally as possible to maximize our investment potential.

News about our business and investment success started to spread. Then, in 2013, we received a phone call from a production company. They wanted to know if they could film a reality show about our lives and business. This was the beginning of a whole new chapter, but it wasn't the chapter we thought was being written.

A production team came out to film our family, and before we knew it, they were pitching the footage to networks in Los Angeles. The response was overwhelming—five different networks wanted to do a reality show about us. TLC made us our first offer. They wanted to do a show called *Twinning*. We still have no idea what that was all about because, in the middle of negotiating with them, HGTV called us.

They told us they had just signed Chip and Joanna Gaines from Waco for a one-hour pilot called *Fixer Upper.* Then they dropped the big news—they wanted to skip the pilot phase with us entirely and jump straight into six one-hour episodes of a show called *Flip It Forward.* They said they planned to feature both of our families and position us as two of the top shows on their network.

They offered us a huge amount of money and, without much hesitation, we signed letters of intent to join HGTV.

But as we soon learned, faith that isn't tested can't be trusted.

## Faith Or Fear

By the time HGTV came knocking, everything seemed to be going great for us—until it wasn't. Long before they ever entered the picture, as our business platform had been growing, our influence had been, too. And with that influence, we openly shared our belief that God's ways aren't just best for building a business or creating wealth; His ways are best in *every* area of life, including the ones society now labels "politically incorrect." These are the very topics Christians are often pressured to avoid or stay silent about.

Meanwhile, our platform was growing. We were invited to speak at events, featured on podcasts, and highlighted in magazines and newspapers. It would've been easy to sit back and enjoy the spotlight, to focus on the growth of our influence. And, to be honest, we had to fight against the natural tendency to protect our reputation rather than stand for truth (more on this in a minute).

But something inside us wouldn't let that happen. There was a fire burning deep down that we couldn't ignore. Sure, we could have avoided the collision with darkness—but doing so would have meant forfeiting the impact we were called to make.

Oswald Chambers once said, "The main characteristic which is the proof of the indwelling Spirit is an amazing tenderness in personal dealing and a blazing truthfulness with regard to God's Word."[5]

Here's a truth you need to remember: while God loves all people, He does not love all ideas.

As believers, we are called to treat every individual with kindness and compassion. But what about the bad ideas—the ones we know are harmful to people? What are we supposed to do with those?

We're not going to tell you what to do. The Bible does that for us:

*"We demolish arguments and every lofty opinion raised against the knowledge of God"* (2 Corinthians 10:5).

The Greek word for "demolish" in this verse means to "destroy as with a wrecking ball."[6] Opinions and ideas that harm human beings should be lovingly met with the "wrecking ball" of truth. Why? Because the knowledge of the truth is the only thing that sets people free.

*"And you will know the truth, and the truth will set you free"* (John 8:32).

If someone is sick, they need a doctor. If they are ignorant, they need a teacher. But if they are captive, they need a warrior! Today, people are being held captive by bad ideas that are keeping them enslaved in sinful lifestyles that harm them. It's time for believers to arise who love people enough to help set them free.

We chose to speak the truth about these hot-button issues, and it didn't take long for the backlash to hit. Almost overnight, we were labeled bigots, haters, and every kind of "-phobic" you can think of. This was back in 2010—long before *"cancel culture"* had become a popular hashtag.

The harshest accusations leveled against us targeted our views on life and marriage. As we shared in chapter three, we were unapologetically pro-life and even started a ministry to support moms in need, which led to us being branded as "anti-women." Additionally, our commitment to standing for God's definition of marriage brought an onslaught of hateful labels—more than we ever could have imagined.

Of course, none of those accusations were true. They were just labels strategically used to silence us and discredit our message. So, by the time we signed Letters of Intent with HGTV, that false narrative was already circulating online. When their attorneys came across it, they quickly raised some concerns.

I (Jason) remember receiving a phone call from the production company explaining that the attorneys had questions about this online narrative. At that moment, I felt fear—a heavy fear—because I realized our platform, and the opportunity to reach millions of homes, was now at risk.

HGTV was talking about putting us in millions of homes—a massive platform we were eager to use to share the hope of Jesus. But now, that opportunity was under threat. It was as if a voice in my head whispered, *"Hold on. If you don't handle this carefully, you could lose the very thing you and your brother have been working so hard for."*

Panic started to creep in, but in the middle of that emotional whirlwind, I fired off a quick prayer—a snap whisper to heaven asking God to bail me out and give me the right words. And wouldn't you know it, He answered. For the next five minutes, I said things I didn't even know I had in me. Honestly, I surprised myself at how good it was! Ha ha.

Essentially, I said, "Listen, we're not anti-anything, no matter what those labels might suggest. We're pro-Jesus, which means we're pro-Bible. We believe that God's blessings are found within His boundaries. If we remove the boundaries, blessings are replaced with burdens. So, if we truly care about people, we can't just talk about living a blessed life—we also need to talk about the boundaries we need to stay inside of to get those blessings."

We set boundaries for our children, don't we? Not because we hate them but because we love them and want them to thrive. We hold firm even when they push back or insist we're being unfair. Why? Because we know that without learning to honor boundaries, the blessings in their lives will eventually be replaced by burdens.

I still remember her response on the call. She said, "Oh, that's good. Most of us at the production company, everyone I know at HGTV, and even your agents—the same ones who represent the Kardashians in Beverly Hills—believe like you do, but none of us are willing to talk about it."

Let that sink in for a moment. These people—many of them outside the "Christian bubble"—share our beliefs, yet they're too afraid to say so publicly. Why? Because they don't want to be vilified online the way we were.

This is exactly how evil operates. It erects a stronghold and then demonizes anyone brave enough to speak against it. It's a tactic designed to silence the truth and keep people in fear.

I hung up the phone and wiped the sweat off my forehead for dodging that bullet.

Or so I thought.

Two weeks passed—no phone calls, emails, or texts from HGTV, our agents, or the production company. I thought we were getting dumped. And I'd never been dumped before, so I had to turn to David for advice! (*That's so lame and not true. –David*)

I remember calling David, saying, "I don't think the attorneys liked my response. I think we're going to lose our show."

He echoed my sentiment, "Yeah, I feel the same way."

So, we got together in our office, knelt down, and prayed. Our prayer sounded something like this: "God, please save our show. Do you have any idea what we're going to do with this show? We're going to use it to tell people about you!"

It sounded more like a negotiation than a prayer.

As we wrapped the prayer, I stood up and said, "Let's write an email to HGTV and try to save our show."

David liked the idea, so he quickly wrote a draft and sent it to me for approval. Here's what it said:

"HGTV, these are our beliefs, and we're never going to back off them…"

Sounds pretty good, right? Well, we weren't done yet.

"…However, when we represent your network in public, we'll be quiet about them."

Now, don't judge me—he wrote it! Ha ha. He wrote it, and I approved it. Here's the scariest part: we both felt a sense of peace about it. But it was a false peace because, at that moment, we were operating out of a fear of man rather than a fear of God.

As a result, we started focusing on the platform we didn't want to lose rather than the Person who put it there in the first place. And anytime you focus on what God has given you—the very thing He wants you to have—and you cling to it tightly, it becomes your idol.

The things you refuse to let go of are the very things that hold you captive.

That's where we found ourselves. We started operating strategically in the mind rather than spiritually in the heart. We were working *for* God, no longer *with* God, because we were fueled by fear rather than faith. All because we stopped focusing on God and started focusing on what we wanted from Him.

Have you ever been there?

We learned that when God gives you something, He wants you to hold it loosely, with open hands, and trust Him. But we didn't see that. We were deaf, blind, and dumb and didn't even know it. Our focus was off.

Well, we didn't send the email to HGTV right away. Instead, we decided to run it by a pastor friend we thought would agree. We knew better than to send it to our dad—we knew what he would say, and we weren't feeling that spiritual. So, we sent it to this pastor instead, hoping for some validation.

Within three minutes, he sent a reply that hit us like a ton of bricks. He said, "How dare you boys write an email like this? This isn't who you are. How do you know that God isn't raising you up for such a time as this? He's not raising you up to have a reality show; He's raising you up to tear down a stronghold that's keeping Christians silent about truth. You don't need to send that email. You boys need to repent!"

How about those apples? That sure wasn't a "seeker sensitive" message, but it was exactly what we needed to hear. At that moment, we could imagine how Peter must have felt when he boldly promised Jesus that he would never deny Him, only to deny Him three times that very night. And when the rooster crowed, Peter was cut to the heart.

That email hit us the same way—it cut us to the heart. Conviction washed over us as we realized we had been operating out of a fear of man rather than a fear of God. And we knew what we had to do. Right then and there, we dropped to our knees and repented for being cowards when God was calling us to be courageous.

From that momentary lapse of faith, we learned a powerful truth: boldness, apart from brokenness, makes a bully. God needed to break us of our fear of man, stripping away anything that kept us from fully trusting Him. He was preparing us for a time when we would need to stand boldly for Him—a time we couldn't yet see coming.

Ultimately, we discovered that the secret to courage is first recognizing your inner coward and then allowing the Holy Spirit to unleash your inner lion. Our *lion moment* was on the horizon, but first, we had to face our *coward moment*—because it prepared us for what was to come.

Thankfully, God forgave us and set us back on course. From that point forward, we were ready for whatever came our way—whether the show happened or not. Either way, our hearts were settled: we would trust God no matter what.

After nearly three weeks of silence, the executive producer called and said, "Guys, are we doing this or what? Let's get filming."

They acknowledged the negative narrative circulating online but assured us they knew it wasn't true and were ready to move forward. HGTV's top executives were on board and eager to get started. To say we were surprised by their enthusiasm would be an understatement. It was amazing to see that they could see past the lies, rise above the noise, and make a fair, objective decision to work with us.

After wrapping up the pilot for *Fixer Upper*, HGTV brought the showrunners from Waco to oversee our show. Before we knew it, the spring of 2014 had arrived, and we were already five weeks into a 10-week filming schedule. Commercials for the show were airing, everything was on track, and the momentum felt unstoppable.

Then, one evening around 9:00 PM, just after finishing our fifth week of filming, David's phone rang. It was the general manager, and her voice was full of excitement.

"Guys, this is great!" she said. "All the advertisers are coming in, and they're loving the direction of your show. But there's a small issue—an activist group out of California isn't so happy. They're upset we gave you a show and are pointing to the online narrative about you."

"But don't worry," she added. "We told them it's a false narrative. We're standing by you because we believe you will be stars on this network."

It felt good to hear that. We went to bed that night, relishing the fact that a company as large as HGTV would stand up for us like that.

## Here We Go!

The following day, we woke up to our phones buzzing with texts from friends all over the country. They asked what was happening with our show and if we'd seen HGTV's Facebook page. We had no idea what they were talking about.

So, we pulled up the page, and there it was—one single sentence at the top: "We are reviewing the Benham Brothers' show." Beneath it were hundreds of comments—vile, hateful remarks about us, our wives, and even our kids. It was shocking and disgusting.

Apparently, the activist group out of California wasn't satisfied with HGTV's support. So they tapped one of their media allies to write a fresh hit piece about the "bigoted Benhams" and blasted it across the internet. The article was published and went viral within hours, shaming HGTV for daring to give us a platform.

By this point, we were considered public figures, and the rules are different for them. You can lie, smear, and spread falsehoods about public figures without facing legal repercussions—something you can't do to private citizens. Sadly, we see this happening all the time in America today, with the mainstream media twisting narratives and spreading outright lies about people. That's exactly what they did to us, painting us as bigoted and hateful fools.

The attacks were relentless, part of a calculated smear campaign. One of the most outrageous claims was that we had stood in front of a mosque shouting, "God hates Muslims." The truth? God loves Muslims, and we've never even set foot in a mosque our entire lives. It was a blatant, malicious lie— fabricated to discredit us and fuel the outrage.

We had no idea how to respond or what to do next. The only thing we knew for sure was that we had a 9:00 AM call time that morning at one of the houses we were remodeling. So, we showed up to the set as planned. While we were getting ready to shoot, my phone buzzed with a text from HGTV's general manager: *"Can you guys hop on a quick call with me and a couple of our executives this morning?"*

"Sure," we replied. We found a quiet spot, put the phone on speaker, and dialed in. The call was brief and straight to the point. "Guys, we're canceling the show," she said.

After I (Jason) got David out of the fetal position and pried his thumb from his mouth, we both took a deep breath. Our first response? "Thank you. Thank you for believing in us." Then we added, "Romans 8:28 says, 'All things work together for good.'"

"I wasn't prepared to be speechless on this call," she responded. "That's very gracious of you both."

The other two executives didn't say a word. One of them was crying.

Our hearts went out to them. We knew this wasn't the decision they wanted to make, but the rest of their executive team felt overwhelmed, as if the weight of the world were crashing down on them. Because of this article, they feared the repercussions of having two guys on their network who openly supported Biblical values.

After the call ended, we sat there in stunned silence. Just like that, the dream we'd been so excited about was over. But deep down, we knew this wasn't the end of the story—God was still writing it.

Later that day, we reached out to the executive team. "We know you believed in us," we said, "but you got bullied into this. There's a Goliath in culture that demands silence from Christians, and we have no intention of backing down."

We had no idea what was coming next, but one thing was certain—we'd already had our "cowardly" moment. Now, it was time to step up and be courageous, no matter what lay ahead.

Word of our firing spread like wildfire, and before we knew it, our phones were flooded with requests from news outlets eager to tell our story. Over the next several months, we conducted close to 200 one-on-one interviews with major networks, including *CNN*, *FOX News*, *Good Morning America*, and *Nightline*.

We were even featured on HBO with Bill Maher, who called us the "nitwit twin brothers" who believe "the same dumb book that millions of Americans believe." At that moment, Christ's words in Luke 21, warning believers about certain persecution, became very real for us. We experienced a level of persecution for our faith that we had never faced before.

The most shocking part, however, was that these groups weren't satisfied with us simply losing our show—they wanted to destroy us completely. They targeted our businesses and even went after our banks. Damaging our reputation wasn't enough for them; they were determined to ruin us financially.

But do you know what felt so good in the middle of all that and still feels amazing to this day? We realized we were spiritually bulletproof—and so are you!

*"For greater is He who is in us than he who is in the world"* (1 John 4:4).

We had *nothing* to fear! Fear is one of Satan's favorite tools—it's how he keeps many Christians paralyzed and silent. We know this because we've felt its grip firsthand. But here's what we discovered: your greatest blessing is often found on the other side of your greatest fear.

So don't back down. Don't let fear dictate your steps. Fix your focus on God—not on the thing you're afraid of losing—and watch what He does.

God wants to move in your life *right now.* He wants to move in this nation. In the wake of Charlie Kirk's tragic assassination, we believe God is ready to raise up a multitude of Bold And Broken witnesses for Christ.

This is not a time for believers to shrink back in fear. It's a time to surge forward by faith.

The world may try to silence you, intimidate you, or even take what you have—but they can't touch what matters most. If you are anchored in Christ, you are spiritually bulletproof. You have nothing to fear.

This is not a time to cower, compromise, or retreat. It's a time to stand firm, rise in faith, and let the light of Jesus blaze through you—whatever the cost. Every act of courage for Christ is indispensable. None are wasted. Each one carries eternal weight.

And as you'll see in the next chapter, sometimes standing strong doesn't look like storming a battlefield—it looks like striking up a conversation at 30,000 feet with a total stranger … or not. I chickened out. My brother, on the other hand, swooped in like he was the in-flight chaplain—Bible in one hand, pretzels in the other.

## CHAPTER FIVE

# MEET ME ON A JET PLANE

*"Evangelism is just one beggar telling
another beggar where to find bread."*
–D. T. Niles

A few years ago, we boarded a plane in Dallas, Texas, headed back home to Charlotte. As usual, we were exhausted. The plane was only half full, so there were plenty of open seats (nobody in the middle!). David and I each had aisle seats with an entire row to ourselves. We could hear the angels singing.

But, as the last passengers boarded the plane a young, college-aged girl came and took the window seat on my (Jason's) row. Let me just tell ya—she was a talker! During the chatter, I felt that familiar battle inside my heart. Part of me cried, "Why couldn't her seat have been next to my idiot brother?!" But deep down, I knew the Holy Spirit was nudging me to engage with her and look for an opportunity to share my faith.

The problem was, I was exhausted. Just before takeoff, right in the middle of this inner tug-of-war, the flight attendant walked up and said, "There's a vacant seat on the exit row. Would you like to take it?"

Uh … do bears poop in the woods? "Absolutely," I said, grabbing my bag before she could change her mind.

Without a second thought, I got up and settled into my new row all by myself. Just before I dozed off I felt that little nudge from the Spirit again. I knew God wanted me to talk with her and bring the spiritual connection she might have needed, but my head was hurting and my eyes were heavy. I needed sleep, you know—I wanted to be refreshed for the kids when I got home. The excuses were endless.

I slept the entire flight home.

When I got off the plane in Charlotte and walked up the jet bridge, I spotted her waiting by the gate agent's desk. She had that look—you know, the kind that says, *I've got something to tell you.*

As I passed by, she looked me square in the eye and said, "Hey, why did you take off like that? I had a lot to talk about." Then she flashed a quick smile, turned, and walked away.

I couldn't tell if she was joking or dead serious, but I've never seen her since to find out. What I do know is this: the second those words left her mouth, my heart sank. God had given me an assignment, and I flat-out refused to do it.

The Lord used her words to rebuke me. I mean, how many young girls say something like that to a forty-plus-year-old man? God got my attention.

"*The Lord disciplines the one he loves, and he chastens everyone He accepts as his son*" (Hebrews 12:6).

The entire ride home I felt guilty. But repentance changes everything. I asked God to forgive me and bring someone else into her life who would listen to what she had to say. I also asked Him to give me another chance, and a few months later He did.

## Fight in Flight

Before Jason got a chance to redeem himself from his epic fail, he and I flew to St. Louis, Missouri, to speak at a pro-life event. I (David) was on the aisle, and Jason got the window. That left the middle seat open for one lucky (or unlucky) person.

I settled into my seat and opened my Bible to study a bit before take-off. Then an older woman came up said she had the seat between us. I noticed she was holding a book with a picture of Donald Trump and a bunch of red letters scribbled all over the cover. I couldn't read what was written, but it didn't look favorable toward him. It was obvious her preferred reading for that flight was quite different from mine.

I stood up and helped her to her seat, and after a little small talk, she looked at me and said, "I just want you to know I'm a flaming liberal feminist who probably thinks nothing like you."

Wow!—now *that's* a great way to engage a conversation. It felt like she smacked me in the teeth without even getting my name. And she looked back and forth at Jason and me while she said it as if to declare, "I'm going to take you *both* down!"

I'm pretty sure it was my Bible that sparked a rise in her, as it has a few times before with folks on other flights.

I'm sure Jason would have been intimidated by what she said if he wasn't already ugly-face snoozing on the window. But I was locked in and ready to engage. In my mind, I was going to dismantle her worldview piece by piece, proving how a Biblical value system was better than a secular one. But I couldn't stop thinking about how abrupt she was and what in her life could've caused her to be so confrontational. My head was ready for conflict, but my heart was pricked with compassion.

I paused a second and whispered a quick prayer for wisdom. I felt the Holy Spirit compel me to ask her questions about her life and family rather than engage in a debate over our different views.

"So, tell me about yourself," I said.

She was clearly caught off guard. I think she had put on her fight face and was ready to duke it out.

"Oh," she said as her face began to calm. "I'm married with two kids and am flying home to be with them."

She then carried on for twenty straight minutes about her family—what they liked to do for fun, how she and her daughter are just like each other, the time her husband caught a big fish on vacation. I didn't even have to ask more questions. She continued talking and then shifted, telling me less about the fun things they've done and more about their struggles.

I just sat there and listened. The more I listened, the more I realized there was a gap in her life that needed to be filled so she could connect with God. At that moment, she didn't need me to change her mind—she needed me to hear her heart. The Lord was about to have an encounter with her.

She eventually told me her son was struggling with depression and anxiety and how it weighed heavy on her. She was also transitioning into a new season in her life, which brought some anxiety for her as well.

I felt a nudge in my spirit say, *Read Psalm 139.*

I asked, "Do you mind if I share a verse with you?"

"Sure," she responded. It's funny how quick and emphatic her response was. Twenty minutes earlier, I'm fairly certain she would've laughed in my face had I asked to read a Bible verse to her.

I opened to Psalm 139 and began reading.

*"For You formed my inward parts;*
*You wove me in my mother's womb.*
*I will give thanks to You,*
*for I am fearfully and wonderfully made;*
*Wonderful are Your works,*
*And my soul knows it very well.*
*My frame was not hidden from You,*
*When I was made in secret,*
*And skillfully wrought in the depths of the earth;*
*Your eyes have seen my unformed substance;*
*And in Your book were all written*
*The days that were ordained for me,*
*When as yet there was not one of them.*
*How precious also are Your thoughts to me, O God!*
*How vast is the sum of them!"* (Psalms 139:13–17)

In the middle of my reading, her chin began to quiver, and soon tears were flowing down her cheeks. I watched her wipe them away while I read. God was speaking directly to her—more than any words I could have formed on my own. At that moment, heaven was invading earth; God was connecting with her in a very real way. It was surreal to watch the Lord move so profoundly. I felt honored to be part of the moment.

I figured I'd better keep reading the rest of the chapter—I didn't really know what else to do—but she stopped me after verse seventeen. "It's weird I'm telling you this," she said as she took out a tissue. "But I was adopted as a newborn and have always felt abandoned by my birth mom. I still have recurring dreams of me at the hospital as a baby, lying in a crib and saying to myself (like an adult would speak), 'Nobody needs to feel sorry for me—I'll take care of myself!'"

It was amazing. She got right to the root of her feminism without me saying a single word about it.

With tears still streaming down her face, she released all that had been pent up in her for years. God's Word softened her as she began to see how much He cared for her, thought about her, and had been with her the whole time she felt so alone. His truth warmed her heart and began melting away the icy coldness built up over the years.

I even started to cry, which is odd for me, as I told her how Jesus had the power to break the chains of abandonment, fear, and anxiety. I shared other Scriptures with her as well and encouraged her to place her trust in God as her Father. She was so touched by the verses, she even pulled out her phone and began making notes about them.

Just before the plane landed, Jason finally woke up from his open-mouthed sleep and joined the conversation. It was nice of him to at least help a little. By the time we pulled up to the gate, she was a completely different woman. The angry, independent, fighter front turned into a loving, caring nurturer. She became so motherly as she asked us about our kids and took a real interest in our families.

The presence of God visited us on the plane that day, and it marked us all. Heaven touched earth. A connection between God and one of His kids took place. This woman who was sandwiched between us left transformed with healing in her heart and a new song in her mouth.

If it were up to me that day, I would have missed that golden opportunity to be a bridge for her to God. I was ready to fight and win. In so doing, I might have proved a point, but I would have lost a person. Thank God the Holy Spirit stopped me in my tracks and shifted my focus.

(If only Jason had been awake to learn this lesson!)

## CHAPTER SIX

# GOING PUBLIC

*"If you wait until you're not afraid to speak,
you'll never speak at all."*
–Unknown

~

As we mentioned in the last chapter, there's no greater way to stand in the gap than by sharing your faith. Sounds simple enough, right? Except it's not. It's far easier said than done. Something deep inside us craves approval, and that desire can push us to stay silent when God is nudging us to speak.

It's one thing to share your faith in a quiet, one-on-one moment, but it's a whole different ballgame when God taps you on the shoulder and asks you to do it publicly. That's when fear reaches a whole new level. Honestly, it makes us wish this verse wasn't in the Bible:

*"If anyone acknowledges me before others, I will also acknowledge him before my Father in heaven"* (Matthew 10:32).

There's nothing quite like the pit in your stomach when you're asked to share your story in front of a crowd, no matter how big or small it is. Your heart starts pounding, your palms start sweating, and every excuse you've ever thought of suddenly sounds pretty reasonable. But here's what we've learned: those moments are often tests. God sets them up to see if we'll obey. And when we do, His power meets us right there.

I (Jason) will never forget experiencing this during my second year of professional baseball with the Frederick Keys, the Class A minor league team for the Baltimore Orioles.

Lots of kids attended the ballpark with their parents for "student night." The place was packed—dads holding a ballpark frank in one hand and a Coke in the other while moms balanced a family-sized popcorn in one hand and little junior in the other—covered with cotton candy.

Just before the game, as we were stretching in right field, one of the marketing assistants jogged over. She looked my way and said, "Hey, Jason. The front office wants you to address the crowd for a few minutes before the game. You good with that?"

*Of course I'm not good with that,* was the first thought that crossed my mind. *Why would I want to go out there an embarrass myself in front of 5,000 strangers?*

Her request caught me off guard. We were literally ten minutes from game time and I had no clue what I should say.

Blame it on a surge of adrenaline in the moment, but I said, "Uh, yeah … I guess," before I could fully process what she just asked.

I think my quick acceptance was a knee-jerk reaction from having just memorized the verse:

*"Always be prepared to give an answer to everyone who asks you to give the reason for the hope that you have"* (1 Peter 3:15).

I should have known a test was coming.

Then she said, "Since it's student night, they want you to speak on the value of reading and studying."

*Well isn't that nice,* I thought. *I can't think of anything more exciting to speak about than that!*

Before I could respond, she said, "You only have a few minutes, so make it quick. You don't have time to preach a sermon or anything."

Funny they thought I would preach just because I was a Christian. This was a few months into the season, so by that time, most everyone knew I was a believer.

Right there, I had a decision to make. Stand in front of everyone and give a little popcorn speech on the value of reading books and studying—a message everyone would soon forget—or let it be known Jesus was Lord of my life—the message no one can ever forget. I knew I didn't have enough time to share the full Gospel, only about sixty seconds.

I jumped up and made my way to the clubhouse. I wanted a few minutes alone to pray before I got out there.

My pregame routine in professional baseball was to find an open bathroom stall in the clubhouse, get down on one knee, and pray. I had already prayed in the stall for this game, but I went in for another round in hopes of a little inspiration for my pregame speech.

"Lord," I said as I kneeled in that bathroom stall, "I need your help. I have no clue what to say. But I know these people need to hear about You. So please give me the words to say."

As I walked out of the clubhouse, my heart was racing. I still didn't know what to say. "God, You've got to come through for me," I whispered, slowly making my way to the field.

The crowd of 5,000 grew silent when I walked toward home plate, the pit in my stomach growing bigger and bigger the quieter it got. Even the other team got quiet as they lined their dugout waiting to hear what I would say.

I was accustomed to walking toward home plate with a bat in my hand and a job to get a hit for the team. But this was a completely different ballgame. I had a microphone in my hand and a job to deliver a message from God.

Dad always told me, "Don't let the butterflies in your stomach keep you from doing what's right. Make them fly in formation!"

As I looked over the crowd, I felt a boldness come over me. It's hard to explain unless you've experienced it yourself. But the minute I grabbed the microphone and looked at the faces of the people in the stadium—the very people I knew God had a message for—I knew exactly what God wanted to say to them.

"I've heard it said," I began, "the most important things in life are the people you meet and the books you read. Well, I'm here to tell you the best book I've ever read is the Holy Bible, and the best person I've ever met is Jesus Christ. He's changed my life, and He'll change yours too if you'll commit to studying His book."

The crowd erupted in applause. People were whistling and parents were yelling, "Way to go!" There must have been a few Christian schools there, because their reactions were as if they were saying, "Finally! Someone just said it!"

There were plenty of people who didn't clap, but at that moment, it didn't bother me. I knew I had the smile of Heaven. God not only helped me overcome my natural inhibition to share my faith publicly, but He also gave me the exact words I needed in just the right moment. I was able to talk about the value of reading and studying, which fulfilled my obligation to the front office. But I was also able to share my faith, which fulfilled my obligation to God.

After the game, I was mobbed with kids and parents. It was normal for kids to get autographs after a game, but what wasn't normal was the number of parents who thanked me for what I said. Many of them mentioned they were thrilled their kids got to see a professional athlete be vocal about his faith.

If they only knew how difficult those ten minutes were leading up to it.

Later, that same marketing assistant approached me. But before she could say anything, I said, "I didn't make anybody in the front office mad, did I? I just couldn't let that opportunity pass."

She replied, "Actually, no. Everyone loved it. Good job." (Phew. Wipe the forehead.)

God gave me an opportunity to share my faith that day, not just with my life but with my mouth. For the newer players on my team, that was the first time they heard me verbalize my faith. They saw my ways, but that night they also got to hear my words.

There have been plenty of times I failed to speak boldly for my faith. But that night became a powerful reminder of what God can do when we simply open our mouths and tell people about Jesus. You never know the lives you're affecting when you do. And like stepping up to the plate in the bottom of the ninth, the swing might feel risky—but when you take it, God meets you with His power and rewards your obedience.

So step up, take your swing, and watch God knock it out of the park.

## CHAPTER SEVEN

# IDENTITY CRISIS

*"When you know who you are,*
*you will not try to be who you are not."*
–John Mason

~~~

The enemy knows something most believers overlook: *identity drives destiny.* How you see yourself determines how you live. If you see yourself as "just" an insurance agent, banker, contractor, or teacher, you'll live like one—punching the clock, chasing the paycheck, and missing the bigger picture. But in God's eyes, you're so much more. It took us a while to understand that, but eventually we got it.

If you've read any of our other books, you already know we played professional baseball before jumping into the business world. I (Jason) had the privilege of playing for a far superior organization than David. He was with the Red Sox, and I was with the Orioles.

Back in the late '90s, while grinding it out on the dusty sandlots of the Minor Leagues, we spent countless hours thinking about life beyond baseball. Cell phones weren't a thing yet, so our deep conversations happened over pay phones in ballpark hallways and crackly locker room landlines.

Those calls weren't just about stats and standings—they were about life. We'd dream out loud about what our futures might hold when the cleats were hung up for good. We talked about raising our families in the same town, building something meaningful together, and using whatever platform God gave us to make an impact.

The Minor Leagues aren't exactly the ideal place to build a stable life or raise a family. So, in 2001, we hung up our cleats and moved our families to Charlotte, NC. With a couple of low-paying jobs and our heads full of dreams, we started over. But one thing never wavered: our goal to work together and build something meaningful.

Interestingly, our first big idea was to launch *Benham Brothers Ministries* and use our platform as former professional athletes to share the message of Jesus. It made sense. Our pastor dad had instilled in us the importance of working for God and spreading His Word wherever life took us.

But there was another drive in us—a desire to make money. Not in a greedy or materialistic way, but more like a desire to do more. We wondered what it would be like to earn a good living and provide abundantly for our families.

But we pushed that desire aside and chose what we thought was the holier path: full-time ministry. We built a website, struck some painfully awkward poses in our baseball uniforms for promotional photos, and wrote a heartfelt support letter to raise funds. Looking back, it's hard not to cringe, but it was the only model we knew at the time.

In our minds, if you loved Jesus and wanted to tell others about Him, full-time vocational ministry was *the* path. That was the box we thought ministry had to fit into. Of course, our understanding of ministry was off—but we didn't realize that yet. We were sincere but also a bit naive.

Yet, just before we mailed out our first batch of support letters, something unexpected happened. As we prayed and dedicated our plans to God, we both felt a deep conviction that this wasn't the path He had for us. Neither of us had peace about moving forward with full-time ministry in that way.

But we still had young families to provide for, and doing *something* felt better than doing nothing. That's when we made a pivot—we decided to start our own business. It wasn't flashy, and we had no guarantees of success, but we did it in faith, having no clue how it would turn out.

We had no business training whatsoever, but we made God a promise. We committed to reading the Bible cover-to-cover each year—from Genesis 1 to Revelation 22—and we would apply anything we learned about how to build and scale a business and how to make investments. That simple commitment paid off big, because in seven years we had built our company into 100 offices in 35 different states.

From there, doors kept opening. We launched businesses in other industries, started investing in real estate, and by God's grace—and a stubborn commitment to biblical principles—we prospered. More than we ever expected.

We tell you this not so you can pat us on the back, but to let you know that, for much of the time we were doing these things, we found ourselves wrestling with an unexpected feeling—*guilt*. We couldn't shake the thought that we weren't in "full-time ministry" and, therefore, weren't doing enough for God.

Until one morning, we stood in front of a packed room of our employees, franchisees, and contractors with our Bibles open, training them on business and wealth-building principles. I (Jason) heard God whisper in my spirit:

*"Who told you that you weren't in full-time ministry?"*

That question may sound odd to you, but it rocked me to the core. It affected David the same way when I told him about it later that day.

As we began to think and pray about it, we discovered that our entire paradigm of *ministry* was off. We didn't realize it then, but we now know we were in full-time ministry the whole time.

We learned that *where we're placed* and *how we're paid* doesn't determine the minister. It's about passion, not position. It's about God's presence in our lives and our desire to glorify Him through our work that makes us full-time ministers right where we are.

This isn't just true about us—it's also true about you.

The devil understands a powerful truth: how you *see* yourself determines how you *behave* yourself. If you see yourself as just an insurance agent, a banker, a contractor, or a teacher, that's exactly how you'll behave. You'll miss the fact that, in God's eyes, you're a full-time minister right where you are. And if you don't see yourself that way, you'll never fully step into the calling God has placed on your life.

God took the scales off our eyes that morning and showed us three paradigm-shifting truths that we now teach believers all over the world:

- You're a minister right where you are.

- You're on mission to bring God glory.

- Your work is worship.

When you know these truths and live them out in your daily life, you'll begin to see God work through you in ways you never imagined. You'll step fully into the identity God created you for—not someone chasing the world at the cost of your soul, but someone standing in the gap, a bridge He can use to connect heaven and earth.

From our paradigm-shifting moment forward, everything changed for us. We no longer operated out of guilt for not *going into* ministry but out of gratitude for *being in* ministry. We understood that ministry wasn't limited to a pulpit; it was happening every day in our place of work. Our sense of failure was replaced with fulfillment as we realized we were right where God wanted us—living as connectors, channeling His truth and love into the places He had called us.

Fueled by our new identity as full-time ministers in the workplace, we slammed our foot on the gas and let our entrepreneurial drive roar. Before long, we were stewarding a family of companies—both for-profit and nonprofit—stretching across the nation and reaching around the globe.

And in every new venture, God made it clear: this wasn't about building businesses. It was about building bridges. It was about Kingdom impact.

Knowing who you are in Christ is powerful. But the real question is: will you stay safe in that identity, or will you risk it to stand in the gap for someone else?

## CHAPTER EIGHT

# A TALE OF THREE PETERS

*"Our greatest glory is not in never failing,
but in rising every time we fail."*
–Confucius

~

The phrase *Bold And Broken* was born out of our study of Peter's life. Peter was likely the oldest disciple—and without question the boldest. He was the only one crazy enough to jump out of the boat and walk on water with Jesus. He was the first to draw a sword when his friends were threatened. And when the other disciples stayed silent, Peter spoke up.

But, as is often the case, our greatest strength can be our greatest weakness. Fortunately for us, the Bible doesn't pull any punches when describing Peter's weaknesses and mess-ups.

Peter was a naturally bold guy. But we see repeatedly in the Gospels how he lacked the genuine humility only a person broken over his or her sin can have—the vital attribute a bold warrior such as Peter desperately needed.

We pick up his story the night Jesus and His disciples had their last meal together, just after the Lord told them He would be betrayed, and they would all fall away. Peter—in his typical bold fashion—declared, "Even if all fall away on account of you, I never will."

Peter couldn't fall away, right? He was the top dog in Christ's inner circle. Of the twelve disciples, he was one of just three who got to see Jesus transfigured on the mountain. He was the one who first recognized Jesus as the Messiah. And he was the guy Christ named as a rock to help build the church. You can tell a lot about people by how they handle a compliment. This one appeared to go to Peter's head because it might have stoked the fire of his inner self-sufficiency.

But Jesus knew what He was doing and where He was going with Peter. He knew Peter's weakness better than Peter did. So, Jesus responded to his bold claim, saying, "Truly I tell you, this very night, before the rooster crows, you will deny me three times."

Peter wasn't buying it. "Even if I have to die with you, I will never disown you" (Matthew 26:31–35).

When we read this story, we can almost see Jesus at that moment, sighing with the thought, *Peter, you have no idea what's coming.*

After they finished dinner, Jesus took His disciples to the Garden of Gethsemane. His betrayal was just moments away, and He wanted to pray. When they arrived, He told the disciples to sit down while He went to another place to pray alone. He then asked His top three guys to come along with Him. Peter was among them again.

Can you imagine how Peter felt? Looking at the last three years with Jesus and considering some of the conversations they'd had, maybe he thought to himself, *Jesus always wants me close to Him. I can't wait to see how amazing it's going to be when He takes the throne of Israel. I wonder what it feels like to be second in command of an entire kingdom. I'll find out soon enough.*

Of course, those thoughts faded pretty fast as he fell fast asleep and started drooling on a rock. As a matter of fact, all three of Jesus's closest buds zonked out hardcore. They couldn't even honor the one thing Christ told them to do—"Keep watch and pray." Nope. Three times this happened.

## Anger—Ditch No. 1

Little did Peter know that allowing his flesh to overrule his spirit was a recipe for disaster. His first lesson was about to play itself out. In the middle of his log-sawing episode, it happened—the enemy Christ warned them about showed up in full force, weapons and all.

Startled awake, Peter grabbed his sword and swung with all his might at the head of one of the men, cutting off his ear. *Not on my watch*, Peter probably thought to himself.

Now, we'll give Peter a hall pass for missing—he'd just been awakened. You'd have terrible aim too. He was probably going for a headshot and hit the ear. He either had a crazy head-rush from just waking up and missed the dude's head or the guy ducked. Either way, it was a swing and a miss.

But this is where the story gets interesting. Jesus told Peter to put his sword away. If you "live by the sword you will die by the sword," Jesus told him (Matthew 26:52). In other words, if we want to take people's heads off, we'll never get their hearts. And *that's* what Jesus was after.

Peter was not yet broken, so in his boldness, he reached for the wrong weapon. He was operating in the physical rather than the spiritual. Thankfully, Christ taught him that instead of trying to *hurt*, we must seek to *heal*. He demonstrated this as He touched the man's ear and restored him.

**This was Peter the bully. He was bold but not broken.**

Operating out of a spirit of anger, he was ready to fight when the mob showed up.

Peter was definitely willing to stand in the gap, but he did it in the wrong spirit, which disqualified him from being the person God could use to bring the plan of Heaven to earth.

## Fear—Ditch No. 2

Yet, Peter still had more to learn because the pendulum of life's lessons often swings from one extreme to the other.

With blood still on his sword, he watched Jesus willingly walk with the mob toward the city. He followed, but this time at a distance. Peter wanted to see what would happen, but he didn't want to be a part of it. No longer was he ready to go all in as he once was. Truth be told, we'd all be tempted to do the same thing.

The mob led Jesus to the house of Caiaphas, the High Priest, who was probably still holding a grudge against Jesus for disrupting his money-making business in the temple, among other things. Standing against the leaders of the day was simply not something you did back then. It got Jesus into a lot of trouble.

While all this happened, Peter sat in the courtyard, warming himself by the fire. Notice how cowardice and comfort replaced courage and commitment when Peter lost his boldness. He was more concerned about staying comfortable than he was about standing with courage.

As the fire crackled and warmed Peter's hands, a servant girl approached and said, "You also were with Jesus of Galilee."

He answered, "I don't know what you're talking about." Liar liar, pants on fire.

Another one approached and said in front of everyone, "This fellow was with Jesus of Nazareth." Peter denied it again, this time more emphatically—"I don't know the man!"

But they weren't buying it, and finally they said, "Surely you are one of them; your accent gives you away."

That's when Peter put the final nail in the coffin as he began to curse along with his denial.

It's as if Peter said, "You still think I'm one of them, huh? Well, I'll prove it to you, you @#%!! I don't know the man!"

We believe one of the most certain ways to disassociate from Jesus is to use profanity. Most people will assume you don't know Him, just like they did with Peter.

At that very moment, a rooster crowed. Peter denied the very man he swore to protect.

"Then Peter remembered the words Jesus spoke: 'Before the rooster crows, you will disown me three times.' And he went outside and wept bitterly" (Matthew 26:69–75).

Peter knew it was over. He failed, miserably. He had just denied his best friend in the world, the man he claimed to be king.

Jesus was put on public trial, humiliated in front of an entire city, flogged, and ultimately crucified. The Gospel doesn't tell us what Peter was doing during this time. We have no idea where he was after he denied Jesus in the courtyard.

**This was Peter the bystander. He was broken but not bold.**

Operating out of a spirit of fear, he was ready to run when the angry mob showed up.

## Time to Get Up!

The next time we hear of Peter came from the angel standing at Christ's empty tomb when he mentioned him by name. He knew Peter needed to be restored from his failure, not destroyed by it. So, the angel said to the three women there, "... He has risen! He is not here. See the place where they laid Him. But go, tell His disciples and PETER ..." (Mark 16:6–7). God is so gracious to us when we mess up.

Can you imagine how Peter felt when these ladies told him the angel mentioned him by name? He was probably thinking, "Wait, I thought I was done. You mean I'm still on the team?"

After Peter checked out the empty tomb for himself, he went back into Jerusalem where the other disciples were hiding. Then, out of the blue, Jesus appeared! All of them freaked out—they thought He was a ghost. But Jesus calmed them down after He showed them His nail-scarred hands and feet.

We know Peter was in the room that day, but we don't have any information that Jesus spoke to him directly. Can you imagine how this felt for Peter? He might have thought, "Uh, are we okay? I mean—I know what you heard me say in the courtyard …"

Awkward.

Jesus was not done with Peter. He showed up again a few days later, this time in Galilee by a lake—the very lake in which Peter decided earlier to go fishing. It's like Peter thought he needed to go back to fishing because his days as a disciple were at an end.

Jesus stood on the shore and called out to him in the same way He did when He'd recruited Peter three years before—"Throw your net to the other side of the boat and you'll find some" (John 21:6). The same result ensued—they caught more fish than they could carry in the net.

Peter realized it was Jesus and jumped out of the boat and swam to shore. Can you sense his urgency? How many of us have hurt someone only to desperately desire to make things right?

Now it was time for Jesus and Peter to talk man to man.

Three times Jesus asked him, "Do you *love* me?" Peter's heart probably felt the sting, reminding him of what he did just days before. All three times, Peter responded the same way, "Yes Lord, you know that I *love* you."

Jesus was teaching Peter the importance of love. No more anger, no more fear—just love for the Savior would enable Peter to be useful to Jesus.

Jesus responded each time to Peter's confession, "Feed My sheep ... Take care of My sheep ... Feed My sheep."

Now, up to this point, Jesus was the Shepherd feeding the sheep; He referred to Himself in this way several times. But now, after Peter's incredible failure, Jesus not only reinstated him but gave him the very mantle He carried—that of a shepherd.

Jesus essentially said to Peter, "You are finally Bold And Broken. So now I commission you to do what I have always done—shepherd people. As I have done so you must also do!" Wow.

Imagine the impact that had on Peter. To fail Jesus like he did but then to be made captain of the team.

## Empowered

In His final words before He was taken back to Heaven, Jesus told Peter and the other disciples to wait in Jerusalem until they were "clothed with power from on high" (Luke 24:49).

Several weeks later, as the disciples were holed up in an upstairs room in Jerusalem, still in danger of being beaten or even killed for believing in Jesus, the moment Jesus told them about happened. It was the Day of Pentecost, when Jews from every nation gathered in Jerusalem, all of them speaking their own dialect. All of a sudden, the sound of a rushing wind filled the room as the Holy Spirit descended upon each of them.

The crowd heard the sound of the wind and gathered where the disciples were. And when they arrived, they were astonished to hear these men speaking in their native languages. Seeing that the crowd was utterly confused, with people wondering how this could be possible, Peter stood to his feet.

Pause here for a moment. Peter could have easily operated out of anger like he did before and scold the crowd without giving them the hope of redemption. They'd killed Jesus, after all. Or he could have stayed seated out of fear of persecution, or because he had been such a failure in the past. But that's not what he did.

Peter stood and addressed them all, speaking in front of thousands of people, knowing full well it could cost him dearly. He did it with a heart full of love for the Savior he'd failed but who had forgiven him and set him back on his feet and enlisted him in His kingdom-building effort here on the earth.

That day 3,000 people got radically saved. Bam! Heaven touched earth through Peter. He went from small and insignificant to strong and indispensable because he was willing to stand in the gap and connect these people to the God who created them.

**This was Peter, the bridge. He was both Bold And Broken.**

Operating out of a spirit of love, he was ready to stand. When the crowd showed up, he didn't run *after* them or run *from* them; he stood *for* them.

Peter finally transformed into the man Jesus always knew he could be—a man willing to stand in the gap so heaven could touch earth through him. God wanted to reach the hearts of people that day, and He did it through a broken man who chose to stand boldly for Him.

Boldness doesn't come naturally. Fear always shows up first. And if we're going to stand strong like Peter, we've got to learn how to face that fear and overcome it.

## CHAPTER NINE

# TAKE ME TO THE WOODSHED

*"Fear knocked at the door.
Faith answered. No one was there."*
–Corrie Ten Boom

B ack in Chapter Four, we told you about our "Peter" moment when fear almost caused us to cave and keep quiet so we wouldn't lose our show. By God's grace, we made it through that test, confessed our weakness, and stood our ground. But the story didn't end there. God had another test waiting, one that came fast on the heels of the first—and this time fear came rushing back stronger than ever.

A few days after HGTV told us they were getting pressure from activist groups, and before we got the boot, we had to film on location at a house we were flipping outside Charlotte. The entire car ride over we prayed, knowing this wasn't just about television anymore—it was spiritual, and we needed God's help more than ever.

When we pulled up to the house, the production crew was already in full motion, running around the house getting things ready. But we quickly noticed something unusual—something we hadn't seen on set before.

In an old beat-up car parked out front, a couple of girls sat staring us down, looking like they were going to jump out of the car and start a shout-down at any moment. They watched our every move as we parked and walked up to the set. We instantly knew these were protestors getting ready to stage some type of demonstration or disruption of the filming.

Here we were all over again, battling fear and thinking, "We're going to lose the show, and people are going to hate us, and this stinks, and oh God please choose someone else." You know the feeling.

We really didn't want these girls to bring our whole production team into the drama. At this point, the crew had no clue about what was happening behind the scenes with HGTV—how they were being pressured to fire us. Fortunately, the girls drove off. We were pretty certain they were simply there to verify we actually had a show and were filming.

## Fear's Effects

We both felt sick to our stomachs. It was clearly just a matter of time before the lid came off and the protests started. The gut ache was bad. So bad we knew that if we didn't get ourselves together, it was going to negatively affect what we needed to do on camera that day. We didn't want to look like a couple of blundering idiots on reality television (although there are a few shows where that's worked out quite nicely for the network).

Isn't it interesting how fear can steal your confidence and cause you to go from feeling like a hero to a zero in the blink of an eye? For that brief moment walking up to the house, knowing full well we were being watched, both of us lost our mojo. Our shoulders were hunched, we weren't talking to anyone—all the joy we typically had on set was gone. Some of the very things that attracted HGTV to us vanished because of fear.

After we got our microphones on, I (Jason) motioned to David to follow me to the backyard. I knew from our past experience with fear the best way to overcome it was to get alone with God and pour our hearts out to Him. If we focused on the problem, fear would *grow* ... but if we focused on the Person (God), fear would *go*.

After turning our mics off, we walked behind a little grey shed out back, got down on our knees, and cried out to God.

"Lord Jesus," we prayed. "We are afraid. We don't want to enter this fight because we know what they're going to do. They're coming after us for our values—for *Your* values. We could get seriously maligned and misrepresented by these people—and we don't want that. Our production company will get bullied and intimidated. HGTV may be picketed. Lord, we don't want this. Please take it away from us."

## Three-Step Prayer

Taking a knee there outside, just out of earshot of the team supporting us, reminded us how it must have felt, at least in a very small way, for Jesus the night He was betrayed. We actually prayed the same prayer He prayed that night:

"... *Father! All things are possible for You; remove this cup from Me; yet not what I will, but what You will*" (Mark 14:36).

This three-step prayer has been something we have held onto for a long time and we've found it's extremely powerful when it comes to facing fear:

1.  **Recognize** God's power—"All things are possible for You."

2.  **Request** what you want or need—"Take this cup from Me."

3.  **Release** it to God—"Yet not what I will, but what You will."

When we got to step one, we felt the stinging conviction that fear was still inside us and it needed to be dealt with. But the more we focused on the power of God, the smaller the problem seemed. We could feel our faith taking over and winning the battle.

In the middle of praying, God spoke a verse into our hearts:

"*One who is wise can go up against the city of the mighty and pull down the stronghold in which they trust*" (Proverbs 21:22).

At first it seemed out of place—what did this verse have to do with fear? But as we asked God for understanding, we heard Him say, *"You're not here to have a reality show. You're here to deal with a spiritual stronghold that's capturing our nation, and I want you to tear it down. Have confidence in Me and do it."*

We haven't had a lot of those, but that was a direct word from the Lord for us at that moment. Fear was growing fast, and God needed to give us courageous faith to overcome it. He did it by bringing clarity to what His plan was for us. We knew then that we could faithfully release this entire thing into His sovereign hands.

## Fear Loses the Fight

We walked behind the shed full of the Spirit (as all believers are), but we walked away from the shed *in the power of the Spirit*. We got "plugged-in" to God and we could feel His power flowing through us. Things were certainly moving in an unexpected direction, and the details of how it was all going to work out were still foggy, but God gave us clarity on our new assignment.

This all took place five days before we were fired. We tell people it was "divine sabotage." God gave us that show not so we could be on reality TV, but so we could be put in the middle of a cultural battle. And that's exactly what eventually happened.

We finished that day of filming with a new sense of purpose and gusto. It was a victory for us—we had confidence and joy. A spirit of fear would not control us. The apostle John said it this way:

*"And this is the victory that has overcome the world: our faith"* (1 John 5:4).

That fearful, downtrodden spirit was gone, and we were back to our old selves again. We weren't overly excited about the conflict we felt God was leading us straight into, but we accepted it without fear.

Looking back, we can see the importance of that prayer behind the shed. It was a pivotal time, preparing us for what lay ahead. We can see now the Lord was calling us to stand in the gap for that moment of time in our culture. This was right at the time when marriage was being redefined and Christian morality was under attack.

But what did that have to do with us? That was the question we asked at first. We didn't want to lose our show or deal with the false perceptions that might come our way if we took a stand. So, we felt paralyzed, like bystanders on the sidelines watching our show drop into the toilet.

For a brief moment, we lost our focus. We stared intently at the thing God put in our hand—the platform of a prime-time reality show—and imagined the increase of our image, influence, and income. That possibility was clearly being threatened. So, our natural reaction was fear to protect what we had.

Like Saul, we hoped hiding "in a tent from Goliath" would protect us until he went away. But God wanted us to operate in faith—like David, whose courage gave him the confidence to stand against a giant.

Those next several days of filming were a blur. And sure enough, five days later, our show was canceled. Yet in the midst of it all, we were able to overcome fear and operate confidently by faith whatever the cost.

Here's the funny part: to this date, years later, people still thank us for not being afraid to stand in the gap for truth. Not afraid? Are you kidding? We were afraid the whole time—we just chose not to be controlled by it. The Holy Spirit filled us with supernatural faith, which overcame our natural fears.

There wasn't an interview we did where we weren't nervous or scared. We found ourselves plenty of times on our knees in a back room or closet somewhere praying and asking God for courage. Each time, He strengthened us to walk by faith and not by fear.

What we learned is that being bold in faith doesn't always have to be dramatic, like David taking out Goliath or Peter preaching to thousands. Sometimes it's as simple as taking a knee when you're fearful, acknowledging His power, and handing the outcome back to Him. Maybe it's saying, "God bless you" to the grocery store bagger, leaving a large tip with "Jesus loves you" on the receipt at the diner, or refusing to let fear about your finances keep you from enjoying time with your family.

Whatever it is, faith is simply choosing not to let fear take control. It's refusing to let fear win and instead acknowledging Who has already won the ultimate battle for our lives.

We've been both amazed and encouraged by the response of believers in the wake of Charlie Kirk's death. Christians are rising up, ready to stand for truth and let their faith in God lead the way. Disciples of Christ are hearing the call to step into the gap.

Will fear come with it? Absolutely. In fact, the very presence of fear is often the sign that it's *your* moment to stand. But don't let fear keep you on the sidelines. Step forward with confidence, no matter how small the task may seem. Fear is faith's greatest enemy, but faith—bold, supernatural faith—is exactly what ushers heaven into earth.

And remember—bold faith doesn't mean you're the biggest or the strongest. It means you know the weapon in your hand is more powerful than anything the enemy carries. Just ask the kid who dropped a giant.

## CHAPTER TEN

# REVERENCE OVER RELEVANCE

*"The remarkable thing about fearing God is that*
*when you fear God, you fear nothing else, whereas*
*if you do not fear God, you fear everything else."*
–Oswald Chambers

For decades, the concept of *relevance* has been a buzzword in Christian circles. Conferences are built around it, strategies are drafted to achieve it, and countless churches have rebranded themselves in pursuit of it. The burning question many leaders ask is: *"How can we be more relevant to the culture around us and still hold on to our convictions?"*

But let's be blunt—this question is short-sighted and weak. When relevance becomes the starting point, we've already lost our way. We begin measuring success by popularity instead of faithfulness and by how many people like us rather than how deeply people trust us. The result isn't spiritual strength but slick performances that entertain yet never transform.

The real question isn't, "How can we stay *relevant* to culture?" but, "How can we stay *reverent* before God?"

Reverence means fearing God more than man—placing His honor above our popularity, His pleasure above the applause of others. It's standing in awe of His holiness rather than bowing to cultural trends.

When we choose reverence, God takes care of our relevance.

Scripture is filled with men and women who made this choice. To their culture, they looked irrelevant—but to God, they were faithful. And that's what changed history.

## Be Like Noah

Take Noah. To his neighbors, he was a relic from another age—a man with strange convictions building a massive boat on dry land. For decades, he preached righteousness while warning of a coming judgment no one had ever seen. He looked foolish. He looked irrelevant. But to God, he was faithful. His reverence didn't just save his family—it preserved the human race.

Hebrews 11:7 says: *"By faith Noah, being warned by God about things not yet seen, in reverence prepared an ark for the salvation of his household, by which he condemned the world, and became an heir of the righteousness which is according to faith."*

God told Noah rain was coming—but rain had never fallen before. Up to that point, the earth was watered by streams and mist from the ground. The very concept of water falling from the sky was unimaginable. Yet for 120 years, Noah obeyed. Every hammer strike was an act of faith.

Imagine the ridicule:

"Hey Noah! What are you doing?"

"Building an ark—God's going to flood the earth."

"What's a flood?"

"Rain—water falling from the sky."

"You're crazy!"

If Noah had chased *relevance*, he never would have built the ark. Because when your eyes are fixed on relevance, you lead with strategy over the Spirit.

Relevance bows to popular opinion. Reverence bows to the Word of God.

Noah chose reverence. He ignored the smirks, the mockery, and the logic of his age. He trusted God when obedience looked ridiculous. And because he did, the ark was built, his family was saved, and humanity was preserved.

But the moment the first drop of rain hit the ground, who became the most relevant man alive?

Noah.

His story proves this truth: *true relevance is a byproduct of reverence.*

When we fix our eyes on God in reverence, He takes care of our relevance to the world around us—in His time and in His way. Noah spent over a century looking foolish to the world around him. But when the skies opened and the flood came, the man everyone mocked became the man everyone needed.

As the saying goes, "In times of chaos, the one who knows what to do becomes the leader."

So we have to ask ourselves: have we become so intimidated by people's disapproval that we've lost sight of God's approval? Obedience is impossible when the fear of man takes center stage.

Relevance gives us no anchor—it drifts with every trend and opinion. But reverence? That's what roots us. It keeps our hearts steady, fixed on the unchanging truth of God's Word.

Relevance asks:

"What do people think?"
"What's popular?"
"What's safe?"

Reverence asks:

"What does God think?"
"What pleases Him?"
"What does He want me to say or do?"

To choose relevance is to fear man. To choose reverence is to fear the Lord. And that's where faithfulness is forged.

Here's the key—when Christians chase after relevance, the result is often the opposite: they become largely irrelevant. Why? Because in the name of staying "relatable," they stop talking about the very things people are actually wrestling with. Like a pastor who avoids what's happening in culture for fear of offending someone, they trade conviction for comfort—and in doing so, they lose their voice.

True relevance doesn't come from avoiding hard truths; it comes from applying God's truth to real life, right where the battle is being fought.

The world isn't starving for catchy slogans or polished marketing. It's starving for believers with backbone and compassion—people willing to step into the war of ideas, to confront error with truth, and to love those trapped in deception.

People need ultimate answers as the floodwaters of culture pound their marriages, families, and faith. Only those anchored in reverence will have an ark strong enough to endure the storm.

## Popular or Powerful

Choosing reverence over relevance will always invite conflict—a clash of opinions and a collision of worldviews. When culture's values contradict God's Word, the reverent believer doesn't bend or blur the lines. Instead, they:

- **Restate:** What does the Bible actually say?

- **Reaffirm:** I believe what the Bible says.

- **Reapply:** I will live by what the Bible says.

This threefold rhythm—restate, reaffirm, reapply—keeps truth alive in every generation and dismantles the lies of the age.[7]

Those obsessed with relevance take a different path. They *reconcile* Scripture to the spirit of the age, lowering God's truth to fit cultural approval. They do this to maintain peace, to avoid rejection, and to be liked. But that's not conviction—it's compromise.

If the Church's goal is to be relevant, it will always be tempted to dilute the Gospel. But if our compass is reverence, the answer is clear: we will speak truth in love, regardless of the cost, and let God handle the results.

Because when the flood rains of life come crashing down, the world won't run to the churches that blended in—they'll run to the ones that stood for truth.

Living this way may not make you *popular*, but it will make you *powerful*. And power with God will always outlast popularity with men.

## Safe!

I (David) remember during my early years of professional baseball when some of the guys would hit the clubs after games. Depending on the city, there were always women waiting to tag along—and nothing good ever came from that combination.

The guys hounded me constantly to join them. Part of me thought, *Maybe I should go—just to build relationships and fit in with the guys.* Isn't that what relevance looks like?

But every time I wrestled with the idea, I knew it wasn't right. There were plenty of ways to bond with my teammates without compromising. I wanted to be relevant, and I knew Jesus was a friend of sinners—but did I really have to *become* like them to reach them?

That question drove me to prayer. The answer was clear: reverence first.

So, I didn't go.

And that's when something amazing happened. When the flood rains of life came—when marriages fell apart, when injuries crushed dreams, when grief broke hearts—guess whose door they knocked on?

Mine.

At two in the morning, I'd hear a knock and find a teammate—drunk, broken, ashamed—pouring out his guilt and asking for prayer. Time after time, I had the privilege of listening, praying, and pointing them back to Jesus.

By the time my pro career ended, I realized something profound: I didn't have to *chase* relevance. By staying reverent to God, I became relevant to these guys when it mattered most.

To this day, I still get messages from former players thanking me for those conversations.

I'm not saying I was a perfect teammate—far from it—but God taught me during that time that relevance is the byproduct of reverence.

## The Final Question

Today, the world is desperate for real answers. It doesn't need Christians who sugarcoat truth or twist Scripture to fit culture's agenda. It needs bold believers—anchored, uncompromising, and full of grace and truth.

God has called you to be that voice—not trendy, but timeless; not popular, but powerful. The only way to do that is to choose reverence first and let Him handle your relevance.

Just as Noah's ark became the vessel of salvation for his family, your reverence can become an ark of hope for those around you who are drowning in the flood of culture.

Noah built an ark to lift people above the rising waters. Today, you can build a bridge to help people find their way back to God.

If you want to stand in that sacred space between heaven and earth, the path is simple: choose reverence over relevance—and start building.

But make no mistake—when you make that choice, the fight will find you. The giants always show up when someone dares to stand for truth. Yet, just like David facing Goliath, you'll discover something powerful: it's not a fair fight. Someone already has the upper hand—and spoiler alert—it's not the giant.

## CHAPTER ELEVEN
# LET'S FIGHT

*"For we do not wrestle against flesh and blood,*
*but against the rulers, against the authorities,*
*against the cosmic powers over this present darkness,*
*against spiritual forces of evil in the heavenly places"*
–Ephesians 6:12

❦

Was the fight between David and Goliath really a fair fight? We all grew up hearing it as the ultimate underdog story—scrappy little shepherd boy takes down the UFC heavyweight champ of the Philistines. But let's slow down and think about it.

Physically, yeah, Goliath had the upper hand. The guy was basically the height of a basketball hoop, with legs like tree trunks, arms like telephone poles, and hands big enough to palm David's entire torso. His armor weighed more than some of the Israelite soldiers. If David had tried to arm-wrestle him, it would've been like a toddler taking on The Rock.

David was just a teenager. No armor. No sword. No helmet. Fresh off the shepherd fields, still wearing his "uniform" with the faint smell of sheep dung trailing behind him. Standing next to Goliath, it didn't look like a fair fight. It looked like a train wreck about to happen.

However, when comparing weapons, David had the upper hand.

Goliath had the spear, the sword, the shield, and the armor of a human tank. But his weapons only worked up close. A spear is a short-range tool—you've got to get within striking distance to use it. Same with a sword. In other words, Goliath's entire advantage depended on intimidation and brute force. He had to bully you into fighting on his terms.

David, on the other hand, had a sling. And in the ancient world, a sling wasn't a child's toy—it was a battlefield weapon. Slingers were the artillery of the day, able to launch stones with pinpoint accuracy from as far as 200 yards. Think of it like the handgun on the battlefield. That meant David never needed to get close. He could drop Goliath before the giant ever had a chance to swing.

Of course the giant fell! The guy with the gun beats the guy with the spear all day, any day.

That's why Paul pulled back the curtain in his letter to the Corinthians and reminded us about the weapons we carry as believers:

*"The weapons we fight with are not the weapons of the world. On the contrary, they have divine power to demolish strongholds* (2 Corinthians 10:4).

Can you imagine stepping into a fight with a weapon so advanced it makes everything else look like a toy? Picture some guy bragging about how he's gonna choke you out, but then you show up holding a galactic laser cannon that can level a city block. That's not even a fair fight. The moment you pull that out, the fight's already over.

That's exactly what you've been given as a believer. Did you know that? Your weapon is *Truth*—with a capital "T." Not "my truth," not "your truth," not the watered-down version our culture pushes. God's Truth. The kind that doesn't bend, doesn't break, and doesn't change with the times.

Satan's weapon is lies. And Truth always beats lies. Light always overcomes darkness. It's never a fair fight.

But it only works if you actually draw your weapon and use it.

## The Raging War Of Ideas

You've seen throughout this book that the fight we're talking about isn't physical—it's spiritual. Our Bold And Broken call is for believers to step up and wage war on this front.

So, where does a spiritual battle actually take place? Not on a field with swords and spears—but in the realm of *ideas*. That's where truth collides with lies, where light pushes back the dark, where God's Word exposes Satan's deception. The war of ideas is no small thing; it's where destinies are formed, cultures are steered, and souls are either set free or chained in captivity.

We touched on this briefly in the introduction and in chapter four, but let's take a deeper look at how Paul teaches us to fight this war:

> "*We demolish arguments and every pretension that sets itself up against the knowledge of God, and we take*

*captive every thought to make it obedient to Christ"*
(2 Corinthians 10:5).

Notice the distinction: ungodly ideas come in two forms—*thoughts* and *arguments*. Thoughts are bad ideas we wrestle with privately in our own minds. Arguments are bad ideas we're pressured to accept publicly in the culture around us.

Paul draws a sharp line between the two. Some ideas we take captive. Other ideas we demolish. Just like in any war: sometimes you capture prisoners; other times you level fortresses. And Paul shows us exactly how to know the difference.

This verse shows us two battlefronts in the raging war of ideas:

- **Privately**—the bad ideas the enemy whispers in your mind, hoping they'll take root and control your thoughts: *You'll never change. God could never use you. Your worth comes from your performance or the approval of others.*

- **Publicly**—the bad ideas that have grown into full-blown arguments, paraded in culture and dressed up as truth: *You can redefine gender, sexuality, or marriage and still find fulfillment. There's no such thing as absolute truth. Follow your heart—it will never steer you wrong.*

Paul gives us a battle plan for both fronts. So let's break them down and see how he calls us to fight—and win.

**On the private front**, when the enemy whispers lies into your mind, Paul says to take the thought *captive*. Notice that he doesn't say "demolish it" (that's for later). You don't have to erase the thought; you just don't let it run free. You throw it in a cell and lock the door. Those lies will still rattle the bars and demand attention, but they don't get to run your life. That's how you strip them of their power.

This is so freeing. It explains why certain thoughts don't just vanish from one day to the next—they tend to hang around. But that's not defeat. That's your opportunity to lean fully on the Lord and keep those lies locked up so they don't run your life. Paul takes it further in Romans 12:2, showing us that victory comes through renewal—replacing the devil's lies with the truth of God's Word.

Our wives live this out. They don't enjoy speaking on stage like we do, but sometimes they're called to it. And when fear starts screaming in their minds, those thoughts aren't destroyed—they're taken captive. Fear doesn't get the last word. God's truth does. And they shine on stage more brightly than we do, every time!

**On the public front**, the strategy shifts. Paul calls these ideas *arguments and pretensions*—lies dressed up as truth and pushed on others. When an idea becomes an argument, it grows into a demand for others to accept it. And if it's a lie that wounds people and drags them away from God, Paul doesn't say to tolerate it or find common ground with it. He says *demolish it.*

As we discussed in chapter four, the Greek word for "demolish" literally means to "destroy as with a wrecking ball." In other words, don't play nice with lies that enslave people. Don't coddle them. Obliterate them.

And here's where the Church often falters. When lies are whispered *privately*, many of us know to take them to God. But when those same lies are paraded *publicly*—when they become arguments shaping policy, education, and culture—we go silent.

We're afraid of being labeled, canceled, or rejected. But silence doesn't neutralize lies; it normalizes them. If David had stayed in the trench with Israel's army while Goliath shouted, the giant would never have fallen.

Back in Genesis 3, Adam's first sin wasn't eating the fruit— it was keeping his mouth shut. He stood by while someone he loved (Eve) entertained a bad idea from the enemy, and he did nothing. His silence was his approval. And that silence cracked the door for sin to flood the world.

We're still paying the price today. The same pattern repeats itself when believers remain silent while lies spread unchecked— whether in our homes, among our friendships, or across our culture. Silence in the face of deception is never neutral. It's surrender. And if Adam's story teaches us anything, it's that passivity in the battle of ideas is just as destructive as outright rebellion.

Christ's interaction with Peter gives us a clear picture of how this plays out in real life. When Jesus explained that He must go to Jerusalem and suffer, Peter—always quick to speak— pulled Him aside and rebuked Him:

*"Never, Lord! This shall never happen to you"* (Matthew 16:22).

That was a bad idea Peter should have taken captive before it ever left his mouth. Instead, he bought into it, turned it into an argument, and tried to push it on Jesus. And how did Jesus respond? He demolished it on the spot:

*"Get behind me, Satan! You are a stumbling block to me; you do not have in mind the things of God, but merely human concerns"* (Matthew 16:23).

Jesus shattered that bad idea right in front of everyone. No soft explanation. No worrying about appearences. Why? Because some ideas aren't meant to be managed—they're meant to be demolished.

## Breaking Strongholds

Here's the real danger: when lies are paraded publicly without a banner of truth raised against them, they become *strongholds*.

In ancient times, a stronghold was a fortified city with high walls, designed to keep enemies out and prisoners in. In the same way, when Satan gets people to believe lies—whether about themselves or about the world around them—he builds mental fortresses. Those lies wall off God's truth, locking people in deception and keeping freedom out.

Strongholds don't just stay in the mind, either. Left unchecked, personal lies spread into cultural arguments, and cultural arguments harden into national ideologies. That's how the enemy turns bondage into law and deception into policy.

This is why Paul doesn't call us to tolerate strongholds but to demolish them. Arguments, left unchallenged, shape nations.

The time for staying quiet has passed. Like David, we've been called to pick up the weapon God has given us, step onto the battlefield of ideas, and face the giant head-on. The giant isn't as strong as he looks—and our weapon is far greater than we realize.

So, when a bad idea shows up in your mind, take it captive—lock it up, refuse to let it control you. It's got no power over you. Replace the lie with truth and you will remain free.

But when a bad idea steps onto the public stage—in your family, community, or workplace—and it's dressed up as truth and demanding applause, don't stay silent. Demolish it with truth.

Here's the key: do it all in love. Show compassion to individuals, but courage against bad ideas. That's how you become the bridge God called you to be. Only the Holy Spirit active in your life can maintain that delicate balance.

The giants of our day may roar through movements, ideologies, and platforms. But just like Goliath, their weapons are heavy, hollow, and built on fear. Our weapon—the Truth of God—carries divine authority. It doesn't just defend. It demolishes.

Make no mistake: you were made for this fight. And when God taps you in, you can rest assured He'll give you the exact truth you need to fight and win.

That's exactly what we were about to find out in our own hometown, when we asked one simple question... and thousands of people confidently shouted the wrong answer in perfect unison.

## CHAPTER TWELVE

# RED LIGHT / GREEN LIGHT

*"When you see injustice and do nothing,
you have chosen the side of the oppressor."*
–Desmond Tutu

We made it to the stage and took our seats as several thousand people stood on the lawn, waiting for the program to begin. We were in Raleigh, North Carolina, just outside the capitol building with several public officials and other invited guests to voice our support for a recently passed bill reinforcing restroom and locker room use to biological sex— men in men's bathrooms and women in women's bathrooms.

We had been invited there as a result of our public stand for Biblical values. They wanted a few "non-political" voices to weigh in.

Protestors gathered at nearly every corner, screaming, "Don't force your beliefs on me," as news cameras swirled all over the place. The view held by those shouting at us was that a person's gender can change based on how they feel at the time. This would mean a forty-year-old male who felt like a sixteen-year-old female should be able to use the women's restroom.

By the time we were announced to speak, the crowd was pretty worked up. All I (David) remember is the minute Jason grabbed the microphone, he said, "On the count of three, I want you all to say the word 'MOP' five times really fast."

The crowd looked at him confused. The lawmakers on the stage had no clue where he was going. But, like everyone else who's been confused by Jason his whole life, they went along with it anyway.

"One—Two—Three," he said.

"MOP, MOP, MOP, MOP, MOP!" the crowd shouted.

"What do you do at a green light?" he asked.

"STOP!" they replied, only to erupt in laughter a few seconds later when they realized what they'd said.

"You can stop at a green light if you want," he said with a smile. "But I think I'll just go!"

Jason's always been riskier than I am when we speak. But I could tell his little humor tactic worked because the crowd looked anxious for an explanation.

"Your brain just told you something that didn't line up with reality," he explained. "Can you imagine what would happen to traffic if just five percent of the drivers in this city decided green meant stop and red meant go? You'd have chaos and not be able to get anywhere."

"Our culture is treating biology the same way," he continued. "God is the One Who created us—that's reality. If we refuse to operate by that reality, it will be like stopping on green and going on red—chaos will be the result. Civil society cannot function without laws based on objective truth."

## What's Your Standard?

Although I hate to admit it, Jason's reasoning made sense to the crowd. They recognized that the minute we allow people to define what's right and wrong for themselves, everything breaks down from there. This is why the Founders of America established our nation "under God," because they properly recognized you cannot build anything apart from an objective, immovable, unchangeable standard of truth.

Good laws are based on an *objective* standard for people's safety, not a *subjective* standard for people's comfort. That's a crucial point to know in these hot-button, cultural conversations.

But we live in a time when "under God" has been exchanged for "without God" because people seek to define their own truth. The idea of an objective standard of right and wrong is not politically correct anymore. Even worse, if people dare to make a truth claim, especially if it comes from the Bible, they're often smeared as haters, bigots, and intolerant.

If you would've told us a few years earlier we'd be called haters for saying a man should use the men's restroom, we would have told you it was more likely for the Dallas Cowboys to change their colors to green and gold and replace the star on their helmets with a big "G." Not a chance!

Although we don't doubt some people have mixed feelings about their gender, redefining an entire system of reality isn't the answer. And although we love those who struggle with these issues, we also cannot sit silently as society disconnects from reality. Changing the traffic lights because a few people aren't comfortable with the color scheme would be disastrous.

In response to this North Carolina law protecting bathrooms, political leaders from other states threatened North Carolina with boycotts and travel bans. Professional athletes and Hollywood stars started weighing in. The NCAA even pulled a sex-segregated sporting event out of our state because we have sex-segregated bathrooms. The hypocrisy was mind-numbing. By the time Bruce Springsteen canceled his concert in North Carolina, we could see the cultural gap widening to a point where we had to take a stand. That's when we got the invitation to speak at the state's capitol.

But we were scared. This was two years after HGTV had shown us the door, and the memory of that firestorm was still fresh. We weren't exactly eager to wade back into another cultural battle and catch the same barrage of insults. And if we're being honest, we were afraid because we flat-out didn't know what to say.

But here's the thing: God always gives you what to say when you're willing to stand for truth. He never leaves His people speechless when they step up to speak for Him.

## Answered Prayer

A few days before the event, while I (David) was up early praying about it, I asked God to give us a word for the crowd. And that's when it came—a gentle whisper in my spirit: *"Traffic lights."*

Of course, when I told Jason about it later, he did what little brothers always do—he stole it. (And just for the record, I'm two minutes older). By the time we got to the event, he ran with the analogy before I even had a chance to open my mouth.

I had no idea what the Lord meant at first. But as I sat with those words—*traffic lights*—God began to open my mind and connect the dots.

I thought about all the cars whisking in and out of traffic on any given day, stopping at lights, waiting for other cars to pass, and then proceeding again. I saw various colors, shapes, and sizes of cars. And I saw all the different people driving them. They were also various colors, shapes, and sizes too, but they also had different beliefs, backgrounds, and views about life. I saw incredible diversity, which was the buzzword being promoted in the news so loudly at the time.

Then it began to make sense. God loves diversity. Heck, He created it! But He also gave us order—laws to govern our actions so we can live together and flourish in society as a diverse people. Traffic works not because everybody agrees on everything— quite the contrary. Traffic works because, despite the incredible diversity of beliefs and backgrounds among the drivers, they all agree on one thing: Red means stop and green means go. There is an objective truth to which everyone submits. The result is we can drive to work or the store or the ballgame—wherever we want—in safety.

As I envisioned the danger of drivers ignoring the objective standard—"red means stop, and green means go"—I could easily see how chaos would erupt in the streets. If all people did what was right in their own eyes, stopping and going whenever they wanted, the once-free flow of traffic would quickly end. The result would no longer be safety but danger. This is tragically illustrated when someone runs a red light and crashes into someone going on green.

We have since used this analogy countless times when talking about the widening gap in our culture. Because today, America has become eerily similar to the time of the judges in the Old Testament when "everyone did what was right in their own eyes."

## Chaos or Calm

Check out what Judges 5:6–8 says, in light of our traffic analogy:

*"In the days of Shamgar son of Anath, and in the days of Jael, people avoided the main roads, and travelers stayed on winding pathways. There were few people left in the villages of Israel—until Deborah arose as a mother for Israel. When Israel chose new gods, war erupted at the city gates."*

A distinct gap in culture existed during this time in Israel's history—a chaotic disconnect between heaven and earth—causing people to literally "avoid the main roads." The result was *war at the city gates.* The Hebrew word used for "war" here literally means "chaos." This happened when people refused to honor the truth of God because they rejected the God of truth, and chaos was the result.

That same spirit of chaos is alive today in the idea of *"my truth."* It sounds empowering, but it's deadly. When everyone clings to their own version of truth, there's no anchor, no standard, no guardrails—just confusion and wreckage. *"My truth"* runs contrary to actual Truth—the kind that comes from God alone. And just like in the days of the judges, when we trade His truth for our own, chaos isn't just possible; it's inevitable.

But the most important part of that passage isn't how chaos erupted—it's about how God chose to calm it. He sent a woman named Deborah to stand in the gap as a mother in Israel, to bring clarity where there was confusion by standing for truth in a culture of lies. She led her nation back to being "under God" and refused to let it remain "without God."

Our primary role as believers is to stand in the *personal gap* by loving people as we reveal to them the Truth that will set them free—the Truth that sets us all free. You've read many of these stories in this book. But we also have the responsibility to stand in the *cultural gap* by connecting God's truth to a disconnected culture. God calls faithful people to stand in this gap like Deborah in her generation.

Although it looks different for each of us, and certainly we don't all have to take the stage in our state's capitol, we can each still lovingly enter the conversation. When God's truth is being trampled and people are suffering, we must.

If we don't, who will?

Too many believers today have stepped off the battlefield, abandoning the roads for fear of being misunderstood, mocked, or labeled. But God is calling us back—calling us to stand in the gap and reconnect His truth to a world that has lost its way. This isn't a time to retreat. It's a time to rise. It's a time to live out the prayer of Jesus: *"Your kingdom come, Your will be done, on earth as it is in heaven."*

God raised up Deborah in her generation, and when the moment came, she refused to shrink back. She stepped into the gap with boldness, but also with love—a fierce love for God and others that drove her to act, no matter the cost.

Now it's our turn to do like Debbie did.

## CHAPTER THIRTEEN

# SAVED & SALTY

*"A private faith that does not act in the face
of oppression is no faith at all."*
–William Wilberforce

⤳

In Chapter Four, we talked about the importance of boundaries and how blessings flow when we honor the ones God has set. Step outside those boundaries, and blessings quickly turn into burdens.

To help keep us within His lines, God placed something inside each of us: a conscience. It's our inner compass—the voice of the Holy Spirit—that convicts us when we're wrong and commends us when we're right, guiding us to stay in bounds.

As individual believers, our job is to listen to that voice and obey it. But as the body of believers—the Church—our calling goes further. We are meant to *be* the conscience of our communities, reminding them of God's truth and pointing them toward His blessing.

Together, we embody what Paul called "*the pillar and support of the truth*" (1 Timothy 3:15). The Church, then, becomes not merely a gathering of the redeemed but the living conscience of society—God's moral voice in a darkened world.

On that foundation, believers are called to remind their communities of what is true, right, and holy—to speak light into confusion and call people back toward the blessing of obedience. That's why Psalm 33:12 says, *"Blessed is the nation whose God is the Lord."*

When cities, states, and nations align with God's design for life, good things happen. And, as believers, we should desire that for the places we call home.

Consider what Jesus said before He ascended into heaven. He commissioned His followers to *"make disciples of all nations"* (Matthew 28:19). This means our mission isn't just to stay clean privately—it's to stand for truth publicly, shaping the culture around us with the truth and grace of God's Word. When we do, entire communities can flourish under the blessing of God.

We do this because we love the places we live and the people who live there—and because when God's people speak truth in love, everyone benefits.

Dr. Martin Luther King Jr. captured it perfectly when he said, *"The Church must be reminded that it is neither the master nor the servant of the state. Rather, it is the conscience of the state."*

Now imagine what your life would look like if your conscience suddenly went dark—no conviction, no restraint, nothing to hold you back from doing whatever you wanted, whenever you wanted. It wouldn't take long for chaos to take over. We need the voice of God active within us to keep our lives in order.

The same is true with the Church. When believers stop serving as the conscience of the culture, society starts to unravel. Darkness rushes in where truth once stood. Without the steady voice of God's people calling culture back to His truth, chaos takes the lead. Just as the conscience keeps a person from self-destruction, the Church keeps a nation from moral collapse.

This is what being *salty* is all about. Jesus didn't save us to blend in or stay silent. He called us to preserve truth, protect what's holy, and point people back to Him. Salt preserves what's good, adds flavor where life's gone bland, and yes, sometimes it stings as it heals. When we lose that edge, we lose our influence.

A believer who's saved but not salty forgets why they were saved in the first place. Even worse, "*...if the salt loses its saltiness, how can it be made salty again? It is no longer good for anything, except to be thrown out and trampled underfoot*" (Matthew 5:13).

Ouch.

## Learning from Lot

Being saved but not salty—that's the story of Lot. Remember him? Abraham's nephew. A righteous man living in an unrighteous city. And not just any city—Sodom. A place so corrupt that God sent angels to wipe it off the map.

Lot was righteous, yes—but his city was not. And that raises a sobering question: if "righteousness exalts a nation," why wasn't Lot's personal righteousness enough to spare Sodom?

Because personal righteousness alone is not enough to redeem a culture.

Peter tells us that Lot was *"greatly distressed by the sensual conduct of the wicked,"* and that *"day after day, he was tormenting his righteous soul over their lawless deeds"* (2 Peter 2:7-8).

In other words, Lot felt the weight of Sodom's sin—but he never confronted it.

We've all felt that same grief in our hearts over the moral decay of America. But God doesn't call His people merely to mourn over sin; He calls us to stand against it. His desire is not for silent sorrow but for courageous truth—truth spoken in love, truth that pushes back the darkness.

That's why Jesus said, *"First remove the log from your own eye, and then you will see clearly to remove the speck from your brother's eye"* (Matthew 7:5).

Christ calls us to live clean *privately*—listening to His Spirit through the voice of our conscience—so we can stand strong *publicly*, seeing clearly and speaking boldly. The goal isn't silence or withdrawal; it's clarity and courage. Because truth, when spoken in love, has the power to set captives free.

In Lot's story, the contrast between private conviction and public silence couldn't be clearer. When the angels arrived in Sodom, they found him sitting at the city gate—the very place of authority and influence. It was where leaders made decisions, business was transacted, and culture was shaped. Lot had a seat there. God's righteous man had influence.

But he hadn't used that influence to shape the city. He was *privately grieved* but *publicly quiet.* He knew the sin around him—he had learned how to live near it without confronting it. So when the angels appeared, Lot immediately begged them not to spend the night in the public square. He knew what kind of evil prowled the streets after dark. He ushered them into his home for safety... and that's when all hell broke loose.

*"Before they had gone to bed, all the men from every part of the city of Sodom—both young and old—surrounded the house and called to Lot, 'Where are the men who came to you tonight? Bring them out to us so that we can have sex with them'"* (Genesis 19:4–5).

Think about that. *All* the men. From *every* part of the city. *Young and old.* Sin had saturated every level of society. This wasn't a fringe movement—it was the mainstream. Corruption had become culture, and the people were proud of it.

Their private perversion had gone public. Their bad ideas had become bold arguments, and now they demanded that Lot—and his guests—participate. That's how sin works. It starts quietly, seeking acceptance. Then it demands celebration. And eventually, it insists on participation. Sin never settles for tolerance—it always demands allegiance.

Lot now faced the very darkness he had long tolerated. The pressure that he once ignored was now pounding at his door. What would he do?

*"Lot went outside to meet them and shut the door behind him and said, 'No, my friends. Don't do this wicked thing'"* (Genesis 19:6–7).

He was right—it was wicked. Lot finally spoke the truth, but only when the danger was unavoidable. He had lived privately righteous but publicly silent for so long that when the moment came to stand, his courage quaked.

And that's when he made a devastating compromise. *"Look, I have two daughters who have never slept with a man. Let me bring them out to you, and you can do what you like with them..."* (Genesis 19:8a).

When you're saved but not salty—righteous in private but passive in public—you end up offering the next generation to the very culture you refused to confront. And you will lose your family in the process.

Lot should have stood in that doorway and declared, "Over my dead body." He should've been willing to die defending truth and protecting his daughters from corruption. But instead, he shrank back. And though God mercifully rescued him, his legacy—his own family—was left in ruins.

As the angels hurried Lot's family out of Sodom, one haunting detail stands out:

*"But Lot's wife looked back, and she became a pillar of salt"* (Genesis 19:26).

Lot's wife became in death what he refused to be in life—*salt*. She turned back toward the very culture God was saving them from, and her story became a warning for generations to come.

Lot's daughters later repeated the very sins their dad refused to confront. They seduced him and gave birth to two nations—the Moabites and the Ammonites—enemies of God's people. It was the bitter fruit of cowardice, the tragic harvest of a man who chose safety over conviction.

## The Call for Today

Parents, pastors, believers—the time for half-measures is over. If we want our children to follow Jesus, we must be willing to stand for truth, even if it costs us everything.

Lot's greatest failure wasn't that he lived in Sodom—it was that he refused to be *salt* in Sodom.

If the Church will not rise to contend in the public square and protect the next generation, our nation will collapse under the weight of its own rebellion. But if we stand—bold, unashamed, and willing to suffer for righteousness—we may yet see God's mercy and His hand of blessing over our land again.

You may feel like Lot—grieved in your righteous soul over the sin surrounding you—but don't *act* like Lot. Don't be saved yet unsalty. God didn't destroy Sodom merely because of its sin; He destroyed it because there weren't even ten righteous people willing to stand (Genesis 18:32).

If we want our children to follow Jesus—if we want our cities, our states, and our nation to be blessed—we must speak truth and be ready to die for it. It would have been better for Lot to fall defending his home than to flee and lose his legacy.

We cannot hand over our sons and daughters to the confusion of a godless culture.

We must plant our feet, lift our voices, and declare with holy resolve, "Over my dead body."

Because righteousness still exalts a nation. Truth still sets people free. And the Word of God still stands forever.

Now is not the time for retreat—it is the time for resolve.

The time to be salt.

The time to be light.

The time to stand.

## CHAPTER FOURTEEN

# THE KIRK EFFECT

*"Our lives begin to end the moment we become
silent about things that matter."*
–Martin Luther King Jr.

～

We can't think of anyone in our generation who stood in the cultural gap more boldly than Charlie Kirk. His mission took him straight into the belly of the progressive beast—college campuses across America—where he confronted error with truth. What began as an effort to persuade students toward conservatism soon grew into something far greater: pointing them to Christ. And for that stand, he ultimately paid the highest price.

As we said earlier, Charlie wasn't perfect. None of us are. He said things we might've said differently, and no doubt he probably wished he'd phrased some things differently himself. That's the reality of living under a camera lens since the age of 18—every word remembered, every misstep magnified. But here's what cannot be denied: his courage, his conviction, and the impact of his life. We don't worship the man, but we do honor the fruit of his legacy—because it continues to inspire a generation to stand boldly for their faith.

In the days after his assassination, grief over Charlie's death hit like a tidal wave. Celebrities, commentators, pastors, and ordinary people—so many who had never even met him—mourned as if they had lost a brother or a son. His death cut deep, crossing lines of politics, nationality, and even religion. For a brief moment, the world stopped and grieved together.

As news of his assassination spread, crowds filled the streets with chants of *"We are Charlie."* Vigils sprang up across cities. Hashtags exploded online. Media personalities who had never shed a tear on camera broke down openly. People who didn't even share Charlie's political or cultural views admitted they were cut to the heart. Why? Because his death touched something deeper than ideology—it struck the soul.

But what stunned us most wasn't just the global response—it was the fire his death lit within the Church. Almost overnight, something shifted. Young believers who had been drifting suddenly began declaring they wanted to go all-in for their faith. Men and women who had been silent about Jesus started speaking openly. Pastors who had been timid found their voices again. It was as if Charlie's sacrifice pulled something dormant out of us all.

We've started calling this *the Kirk Effect.* But it's more than a phrase—it's a movement. It's not about a personality; it's about a people. It's about what happens when the boldness and brokenness of one man ignites the hearts of thousands. And as we've watched this ripple across nations, we've noticed two undeniable marks of the Kirk Effect:

- People want to go deeper with the Lord

- People want to stand stronger for Him

## Go Deep

The first wave of the Kirk Effect has been a hunger for God. When tragedy strikes, we often see people fall to their knees in prayer, but what's happening here feels different. This isn't just momentary grief; it's an awakening.

Across campuses, churches, and city squares, prayer meetings are swelling. Not the polished kind with cool programs and tidy schedules, but raw, unfiltered gatherings where people are crying out to God with everything they have.

Charlie's death has reminded us that we are in a very real spiritual battle. What happened to him was a spiritual war manifested in the flesh. And if it could happen to him, it could happen to any one of us. So if we're going to win, we need God more now than ever. The fight is already at our doorstep.

That reality is driving believers to run back to God's presence with urgency. People who once dabbled in faith are now diving in headfirst. The Bible is no longer just another book on the shelf—it's become their weapon and daily bread. Worship is no longer just a Sunday setlist—it's become a lifeline on the battlefield.

We've heard testimonies of young men who tossed out their addictions, young women who walked away from toxic relationships, and entire friend groups who decided to start meeting weekly to study Scripture and pray. Why? Because the Kirk Effect awakened something inside us that said, "I can't live halfway anymore. If Charlie was willing to die for Christ, then I can live for Him."

This hunger is what revival looks like at its core—not emotional hype, but a deep yearning for God Himself. And as believers press in, the depth of their relationship with Him is growing like never before.

## Stand Strong

The second mark of the Kirk Effect is courage. It's not just that people want to know God more; it's that they want to be useful for Him in the great spiritual battle that rages in the nation. They want to stand boldly for their faith, whatever the cost.

Charlie's life was marked by boldness. He stood in spaces where most believers would shrink back. He didn't always say things perfectly, but he said them courageously. And now, in the wake of his death, that courage is spreading.

We've seen students walking onto their campuses with a Bible in hand, starting conversations they used to avoid. We've heard of employees taking their faith into the workplace, no longer hiding what they believe. Pastors are preaching with fire again, unafraid of who might walk out or what criticism might come. Even Vice President J.D. Vance said at Charlie's memorial service, "I have talked more about Jesus Christ in the past two weeks than I have my entire time in public life."

The Kirk Effect!

It's as if Charlie's final act was to hand us all a torch, daring us to carry it forward. His death confronted us with a sobering truth: if speaking truth could cost him his life, what excuse do we have for staying silent? And instead of shrinking back in fear, thousands are surging forward by faith.

This is what happens when boldness spreads through a generation. People stop living for applause and start living for conviction. They stop measuring their worth by likes and followers and start measuring it by faithfulness to God. They stop bowing to the spirit of the age and start standing firm in the Spirit of Christ.

And here's the beauty—this boldness isn't brash or arrogant. It's boldness anchored in brokenness. It's not about yelling louder, it's about loving deeper. It's not about winning arguments; it's about winning souls. This is why the Kirk Effect is so powerful—because it's producing believers who are both unshakable and compassionate, both courageous and tender.

## Be The Bridge

And this brings us back to the theme of *Bold And Broken*. The Kirk Effect isn't just about stirring emotions or sparking courage—it's about believers becoming bridges, carrying God's love and truth to those still disconnected from Him. Bridges are built when boldness is laid on the foundation of brokenness. That's what Charlie modeled, and that's what God is calling us into now.

And it's not just Charlie—his wife Erika modeled the Bold And Broken life! She has shown amazing boldness, refusing to be bullied by the media and let those who want to silence the truth win the day. At the same time, she's shown incredible brokenness by choosing to forgive the man who killed her husband—on live TV! Only a person standing in boldness on the foundation of brokenness could do something like that.

When people choose to forgive and walk in humility, they anchor themselves in God's presence—that's brokenness. When they stand strong for Him, they carry His truth into the world— that's boldness. And when those two come together, believers become bridges between heaven and earth.

That's what the world needs most right now—not more walls of division, not more noise of outrage, but bridges. Bridges that connect people to the love of God. Bridges that carry truth across the chasm of lies. Bridges that invite the lost and the broken into the hope of Christ.

This is the heartbeat of the Kirk Effect. It's not about idolizing a man; it's about imitating his courage, his conviction, and his willingness to let God use his life. His death was not the end of his influence; it was the beginning of a movement. And that movement is calling all of us to rise.

## The Invitation

So, what do we do with the Kirk Effect? We don't just observe it. We don't just applaud it. We step into it.

For some, that means carving out time to seek God in ways you never have before. Shut the door, open your Bible, and refuse to move until His Word grips your heart. For others, it means opening your mouth in spaces where you've been silent.

Speak truth in love at work, at school, in your family. Don't shrink back. Don't apologize for standing with Jesus.

The Kirk Effect is sweeping across the globe, but movements are only as strong as the individuals who answer the call. Will you go deeper with the Lord? Will you stand strong for Him? Will you let your life become a bridge that others can walk across to meet the living God?

The world doesn't need more spectators. It doesn't need more half-hearted believers. It needs bridges—men and women willing to stand in the gap, carrying the presence of God into a world desperate for hope.

This is the Kirk Effect. And this is your invitation.

## CHAPTER FIFTEEN

# A PACKED LUNCH

*"Faithfulness in little things is a big thing."*
–St. John Chrysostom

C harlie Kirk stood in the cultural gap, taking arrows on the frontlines of a national battle. But not everyone is called to that kind of stage. Sometimes standing in the gap looks a lot quieter, and a lot closer to home.

For our mom, it wasn't about college campuses or news headlines. It was about deli sandwiches and an oversized bag of chips. To us, faithfulness may have looked like witnessing to a stranger on a plane or standing strong against cancel culture, but to her, it looked like making sure her boys had lunch every single day.

And here's the beauty—God is just as pleased with a mom faithfully packing lunches as He is with a man boldly facing down culture on the national stage. Because in His Kingdom, it's not the size of the platform that matters, but the faithfulness of the person standing in the gap.

"I'll trade you for your lunch."

We heard those six words repeated probably a thousand times in high school (well, maybe not a thousand, but a lot). The reason for this was our mom took our school lunches seriously. So seriously we rarely went to school with a packed lunch. Mom made and delivered our lunches from scratch every day. Call us spoiled or whatever you want—we don't care—because our mom knew how to show love to her hungry puppies.

From the moment our screen door slapped behind us in the morning to thirty minutes before the noon lunch bell, our mom was at home working away in our closet-sized kitchen, whipping up a lunch fit for King Solomon's table. Although she didn't have the budget of a king, she put together some of the best lunches two growing boys could ever have—all neatly packed into Tupperware containers.

When 11:30 a.m. rolled around, the hunger hounds in our teenage stomachs moved from barking to straight up howling. The minute we heard the lunch bell ring, we'd dart outside, shaking with anticipation to see what Mom concocted. We couldn't wait to see her.

We lived only a mile from our school—Garland Christian Academy—so Mom would pack away all her little Tupperware containers into a big cardboard box, put our little brother and sister (Johnny and Abby) in their double stroller, and walk our lunch to school. Whichever kid sat in the front held the box.

This was no small shoebox either. It was big enough to fit about four shoeboxes. And we were NEVER allowed to throw it away. That was mom's box. If even the thought of throwing it in the dumpster crossed our minds, she might have gone on lunch-making strike. She loved her box.

Like clockwork, at 11:30 a.m. Mom and the kids would round the corner of our parking lot and stroll through the rows of cars with an aroma of goodness in tow. And, like clockwork, the two of us along with a handful of friends would run out to greet them.

## Feeding Her Boys

Our buddies knew to stay away from our lunch. If any of them even thought about touching that box, it was not going to end well for them. I (Jason) think Josh Stanberry got an ear full of Cheetos one day—but I don't really remember.

(Do you ever have random thoughts such as, "I wonder what that stranger at the table next to me would think if I chewed up this crab cake and blew it into his ear," or "Do you think that guy would be mad if I stirred his shrimp-n-grits with my finger?" Well, the high school lunchroom is where you execute thoughts like that. And we had a few buddies who were on the receiving end.)

Mom would hand off the box while our friends hugged her and the kids. She'd have this big smile on her face like she just ran a race and came out victorious. She never really said much, but we could tell from the look on her face she loved doing it. This, to her, was living—and it was a way she brought a little bit of heaven into our lives.

Looking back, we can see this simple act of faithfulness fueled our mom—to know her boys were taken care of and she was appreciated for it. That's it—so simple, but so powerful. She wasn't trying to save the world; she was just faithful right where God placed her and to the people He put in her life.

## Unsung Hero

It reminds us of the unsung hero in all four Gospels where Jesus fed the 5,000. After He'd been preaching all day, His disciples told Him to send the people away so they could get food, which was probably more *their* desire than it was the crowds'—because the people were hanging on His every word.

We can just hear the disciples now, "Dude, I'm starving! When do you think He's going to be done? Who wants to tell Him to wrap this thing up?" (Jason: If David were around, he would've been leading that charge.)

But Jesus, always one step ahead of His guys, responded, "Why don't *you* give them something to eat."

Boom. The disciples saw the need, and Jesus saw the opportunity—for heaven to touch earth through *them*. The hunger of the crowd became a moment for Jesus to practically manifest through His disciples, "Thy kingdom come, Thy will be done, on earth as it is in heaven."

But how? How could these guys provide enough food for that many people? It would take six month's income to buy enough bread just for everyone to have a bite. It was an impossible situation—there was no way they could execute what Christ told them to do. Not even a chance.

Of course, we have the luxury to see how it all worked out, but they didn't. They had no clue what was coming. The more they focused on the problem, the bigger the problem got. But the minute they looked to the Person, Jesus, the solution to their problem presented itself.

"What do you have?" Jesus asked.

The account in the Gospel of John tells us that, after searching the crowd, Andrew found a little boy who had five small loaves and two fish—enough for a few tuna fish sandwiches.

Jesus took the loaves and fish, prayed over them in front of the crowd, and after breaking the loaves, He told the disciples to distribute them to the crowd. And the more food they gave away, the more food they had—it was incredible. Twelve full baskets later, the crowd was fed, and the disciples had leftovers.

Heaven touched earth in that moment as these hungry people had an encounter with the power of God, all because a little boy was willing to give Jesus what little he had. He'd showed up with enough food for himself and possibly a friend. But after Jesus got ahold of what he had, it was enough to feed thousands.

## Who Packed Your Lunch?

The story is good enough if we just leave it at that. But we believe the unsung hero of this miracle was not the disciples or even this little boy—it was the boy's mother. There were probably a lot of kids in the crowd that day, but one kid's mom packed a lunch.

We can imagine earlier that day the little guy running into the house to tell his mom Jesus was coming through town. "Can I go see him, Mom? Please let me go!"

"Sure, that will be fine," she responds. "But you're not going anywhere until I pack you a lunch."

This mother, whom we never got to see and whose name never found its way into the Bible narrative, packed a lunch that became the seed for an incredible miracle. She became the unseen hero of one of the greatest miracles in recorded history. She had no idea the lunch she packed for her boy would be unpacked by the Savior of the world.

## Rivers

Oswald Chambers once said, "A river touches places that its source knows nothing of." This mom was the source for her boy, and he was able to touch the lives of more than 5,000 people when he gave what he had to Jesus.

To us, this mom was a bridge—an unsung hero who brought divine connection so the work could get done. She packed a lunch privately so Christ could unpack it publicly. Heaven connected to earth that day, and peoples' lives were radically changed because Momma was faithful to simply pack a lunch.

So often in today's culture, simple acts of faithfulness like this are minimized and not recognized, but Jesus can use them to do incredible miracles. Our mom touched our lives, and we're still talking about her faithfulness today. She's not with us anymore, but we'll never forget her faithfulness, even when nobody else was watching. We know she was greeted in heaven with a host of witnesses who hugged on her, much like we used to in that old high school parking lot. We can see the smile on her face right now as she tells them, "Wait 'till you meet my boys!"

When we encourage believers to stand in the gap, we do it with an eye to our mom—the faithful saint who made an indelible impact on our lives. What God has done with us publicly is simply a testimony of what she did for us privately. And now here we are giving her the public recognition she deserves.

Hats off to you, Mom!

## CHAPTER SIXTEEN

# KNEELING IN THE GAP

*"You are the only Bible some unbelievers
will ever read. So live with such boldness that
they cannot miss the Author."*
–Unknown

∽

If being Bold And Broken makes us bridges between heaven and earth, then prayer is the foundation under that bridge. Before you can truly stand in the gap, you must first kneel in the gap—because every battle won in public is first fought and won in private, alone with God.

Prayer connects the chaos of earth to the calm of heaven, aligning our hearts with His will and unleashing His strength into impossible situations. Without it, our boldness turns into bluster and our brokenness turns into despair. But with it, heaven invades earth.

One of the clearest pictures of this comes from one of our favorite family movies, *War Room,* by Alex and Stephen Kendrick. Our kids often beg us to play it on road trips, and we're always glad to say yes, because it's more than just entertainment. It's a vivid reminder of the power of prayer and why it matters so much for anyone who wants to stand in the gap.

In the movie, an older woman, Miss Clara, teaches a struggling wife how to pray—how to create a war room of prayer where she does battle on her knees against the spiritual forces of darkness, especially those tearing her marriage apart. The final scene ends with Miss Clara in her own war room—a small closet in her house—on her knees crying out to God to raise up a generation of believers who will do battle for the Lord.

"Raise 'em up, Lord, raise 'em up!" Miss Clara prays. "Raise up warriors, Lord, who will fight on their knees!"

If you haven't seen the movie, you should. There's no doubt it will energize your prayer life. Your kids will love it, too, and the prayer at the end will blow your hair back.

## *War Room* in Our Own Backyard

Interestingly, the movie was filmed in our hometown of Concord, North Carolina. We've been friends with the Kendrick brothers for years, so when they were looking for a place to film their next movie, we pitched the idea of filming it here. Well, maybe we didn't pitch the idea as much as we threatened them—"You'll film the movie here or we will punch you both in the face." Just kidding! But they did eventually cave and brought the entire movie production here in the summer of 2014.

A movie on prayer filmed in our hometown meant more to us than anyone involved ever really knew. We moved to Concord in the early 2000s just after ending our career in professional baseball because of a man who had his own war room—a man who changed the direction of our lives forever.

He lived out the *War Room* life, especially the final scene where Miss Clara was on her knees crying out to God. That scene was an exact picture of what this man did every single morning, in Concord, just a few miles from where Miss Clara's prayer scene was filmed. Never before had we seen a man of prayer quite like him. Never had we been around someone who fought God's battles on his knees with such spiritual power and tenacity.

## Flashback to College Days

We met this prayer warrior in the fall of 1997. We were juniors at Liberty University, and we spent Thanksgiving in Atlanta, Georgia, with our extended family. We spent four straight days indulging our appetites for both food and football. We consoled ourselves by saying we were simply working on our "before pictures" for our New Years fitness resolutions.

While we were in Atlanta, our dad told us he wanted us to meet this real estate tycoon who was doing amazing things for the Lord in Concord.

"His name is David Drye," he said. "He flew me in to speak to his company and the school and be on his show."

Evidently, this guy was a successful businessman who started a Christian school and hosted a Christian television show. Mr. Drye lived in Concord, which just happened to be on our way back from Atlanta to Liberty. When Dad told him we'd be passing through, he invited us to spend the night at his house on Sunday night and then speak to his team on Monday morning.

We showed up that Sunday night and quickly realized our dad seriously underplayed Mr. Drye's business success. From the enormity of his house and size of his property, it was clear he experienced a level of financial success beyond anything we'd ever seen. Our first thoughts were, "What kind of business does this guy have, and how can we get involved?"

We walked up the brick steps and were greeted by a bright-smiling fifty-year-old man who beamed with excitement. "I'm so glad you guys are here," he said. "Come in and meet my family."

We had never been in a house quite like that in all our lives. By the time we stopped gasping at the magnitude of the place, we noticed a bunch of kids sitting on couches in the living room, eating. They were the five youngest of his eight children.

"You guys want a Mr. C's burger?" he asked. "These things are famous around here."

Asking a couple starving college guys if they would like to eat burgers is like asking if fat puppies like big bones. Of course, they do! There's no need to ask.

After indulging in a few Mr. C's burgers and confirming they were worthy of the "famous" tag, we followed Mr. Drye upstairs to our room for the night. He put us in his boy's room, just down the hall from his office. We were bummed we had to take the stairs instead of the elevator—apparently, he wanted us to get a workout.

"Breakfast is at 7:00 a.m.," he said. "We've got a big day planned for tomorrow."

As we lay there in the darkened silence of that room, we quietly marveled at how successful this man was. We were raised by a preacher in a lower-middle-class family, and most Christians we knew were like us. We didn't run in circles with people like this guy.

We drifted off to sleep in the amazing comfort of beds that far exceeded our twin-sized mattresses back at the dorm room in Liberty. Then, at 4:30 a.m., we were startled awake by the sound of someone yelling down the hall.

## Awake at Dawn

"Dude! What's that?" We both got up and crept to the door, cracked it open, and looked down the long, dark hallway. We could see light coming out from under the door of Mr. Drye's office. As we stood there with bated breath and hearts pounding, we realized he wasn't yelling—he was praying.

For the next hour, we heard him pouring his heart out to the Lord and doing battle with the enemy. He would go from telling God how much he loved Him to rebuking the devil in the name of Jesus. "You have no authority over my family or my business, devil!" he shouted. "Get away from them!"

We grew up in a family that believed in prayer and put that belief into practice. But this was a whole new level—never before had we seen such emphatic prayer. This man was on his knees in hand-to-hand combat with the devil.

Fortunately, we were able to fall back asleep for about an hour. The next morning, after polishing off an insanely good breakfast, we were whisked away in his Suburban to his office where we were set to speak to his staff. On the way, we asked dozens of questions about how he started the business.

## The Mission

"I began in insurance," he said. "But then I realized I wanted to create something that could make millions of dollars to fund God's work on the earth. So, I got into real estate."

Whoa. We had never heard anyone talk like that before. A person who wanted to make millions of dollars to give away?

Before we could get the next question out of our mouths, we pulled up to a big white building with "David Drye Company" on the marquee sign out front. We walked into the foyer and up the stairs to a large conference room where about thirty people were gathered, waiting for Mr. Drye—and us.

*This guy has thirty employees? That's huge!* We quickly found out these people were only a few of his leaders and direct support staff. His company had nearly 400 employees who managed forty-three apartment complexes across two states.

We spent the whole day with him as he hauled us from one speaking engagement to the next. The longer we were with him, the more impressed and inspired we became. We probably asked him no fewer than 100 questions. We couldn't drive more than two or three miles without him pointing out another apartment complex he owned, or a fun-park he opened, or an office complex he built. And the whole time, he explained that his entire business was built upon prayer.

"I have prayed for the last twenty years that God would bless my business," he said. "I shout, 'God, bust those rocks and break those chains that hold back your blessing from me. I commit my way to you. Give me more that I may bless you with it!' Boys, God has answered my prayers."

While he was talking, his fists were balled up and swinging wildly. He was a pretty passionate guy. And he had no idea how to wait until his truck came to a complete stop before he changed gears. He'd back out of a parking spot at warp speed and slam it into drive before he even pushed the break. It was an adventurous ride that day—in more ways than one.

At the end of the day as we were driving back to his house, he asked if we wouldn't mind flying back to Liberty in his helicopter since he didn't have time to drive us back.

"Uh, are you kidding? That would be amazing!" (We might have only thought the first part.) We had never been in a helicopter before.

When we pulled onto the half-mile-long driveway at his house, he reached in his pocket and pulled out a small, worn piece of paper. "Do you boys know what this is?" he asked.

"No, Sir," we said.

"On this sheet of paper," he continued, "I've written goals for my family and my business. When you guys heard me this morning, I was laying my hands on these goals and asking God to help me accomplish everything on the list. But I know Satan doesn't want me to succeed, so when I pray I know I've entered a battlefield in the spiritual realm. I wage war in the spirit before I go to war in business."

As he was talking, he handed us the piece of paper. "Take a look," he said. "I want you to see what I've written on there. I don't usually do this, but I feel the Lord wants me to let you see."

We couldn't get past the first point:

"Give away $1 million a month from my business."

We had never seen numbers like that before, much less written on a piece of paper and prayed over by a man who was well on his way to accomplishing it (if he hadn't already). He handed it to a couple broke college kids who barely knew how they were going to fill their truck with gas. But the Lord told him to show it to us. We're glad he did. What stuck out most was that his first goal revealed the amount he wanted to give away—90%.

He looked at us with penetrating eyes. "Boys, I believe God has a great plan for both of you," he said. "But that plan is only going to go as far as your prayer life is deep. You need to go after God in prayer like never before. Make big goals for yourselves spiritually and financially and then go after them until He either grants your request or changes what you should ask for."

When we gave the paper back to him, he asked us something that changed the trajectory of our lives. "When baseball is over," he said, "would you consider coming to work for me, so I can teach you what I know? I've been praying for God to spark a revival in America right here from Concord, and I want to pour myself into young men like you."

Uh, do bears poop in the woods? We responded with an emphatic "Yes!" David Drye gave us a vision for life after baseball. To be part of a thriving business led by a man with a heart to change the world for Christ—now *that* was magnetizing.

Just before we left, he opened the tailgate of his suburban, reached his hand into one of the several boxes inside, and handed us each a copy of the autobiography of George Mueller. "Aside from the Bible, this is the best book I've ever read," he told us. "I give them out to everyone I can. I have modeled my prayer life after this great man, and you should too."

Inside each book was his business card. The front of the card just said "Jesus Loves You" in big red letters. On the back was his contact information. It was a simple way to let people know what was most important in his life.

We prayed together and then said goodbye.

Our heads were buzzing on the flight back to Liberty, not just because we were stoked to be flying in a helicopter but because we felt this could be one of the most life-changing days of our lives. We had no idea what the future held, but finally, we had a vision for life after baseball and a powerful prayer life to go with it.

The pilot landed in the outfield of our baseball stadium. Talk about the best thing that could happen to a couple of college athletes—we looked like big wigs getting off that thing and running with our heads down. It was like a scene from a movie.

## The Impact

Our prayer lives changed that day. From that point forward, we began to pray bold prayers like we'd never prayed before, recognizing prayer is a battle and we are to wage war on our knees. We also read the book. If you haven't read about the life of George Mueller, it's a must-read. Put his autobiography on your list. It's in our top five books of all time.

A year later, we were both drafted into professional baseball—David by the Red Sox and me (Jason) by the Orioles. In my second year as a minor leaguer for the Orioles, I broke my leg in Hickory, North Carolina. We tell the story in detail in our book *Miracle in Shreveport*. It was an epic break, one that required emergency surgery and several days in the hospital.

Because it was the final game of a seven-day road trip, our team couldn't wait for me, so they left me behind and headed home. By the time I got out of surgery, I was stuck by myself in Hickory, alone in a hospital room.

The next morning, after I finished breakfast, I heard a knock at the door. "Come in," I said, wondering who in the world it could be. To my total amazement, it was David Drye and one of his sons. We hadn't seen each other in two years.

"We heard about what happened to you and we came to pray for your healing," he said with a huge smile on his face. "You didn't think you could be so close to us and I wouldn't come see you, did you?" Hickory was less than an hour from Concord.

"How did you hear?" I asked.

"Your dad called last night to ask for prayer," he said. "So I told him I would do even better—I'd come pray for you in person."

I was so thankful to see a familiar face. I was even more thankful it was a man who prayed like him.

As we were talking together, he gave out his "Jesus Loves You" business card to every nurse or doctor who came into the room. Then he placed one in the picture frame on the wall in front of my bed. I looked at that thing every day that I was in the hospital.

After we prayed together, I said, "I just gotta ask—did you fly your helicopter here?"

He smiled big. "Yep. Landed it on the roof."

He then asked if I'd read the book on George Mueller. I told him I did and how it definitely lived up to the hype. He said he'd send me a case full of them so I could give them to the guys on my team.

He then reminded me that he wanted David and me to come work with him when baseball was over. "That's a deal," I said.

He leaned over and hugged me in bed. When he walked out of the room, I was struck with the feeling that this was one of the greatest human beings I met in my life. I remember thinking it would be nice to be like him one day.

One month later, I was recovering in Dallas at my parents' house when we got a phone call.

"David Drye and his wife Ann were just killed in a plane crash," the voice on the other line said.

I lost my breath.

They had been on his private plane headed to their beach house when one of the engines failed. The pilot almost made it back to the runway, but their wing clipped a tree and the plane flipped upside down. The pilot, David and Ann, and one of their senior leaders all died that day.

I couldn't believe what I heard. "There's no way—just no way he's gone," I thought. My mind was racing a million directions. I had put so much hope into a future with Mr. Drye, and he was gone. "His family. His business. Lord help them," I prayed.

Two days later and still in shock from that phone call I received, a package arrived from Concord. I opened it, and there was the case of George Mueller books Mr. Drye had promised to send. On top was a scribbled note in his handwriting:

"Have fun giving these out. Let's talk soon.—David Drye"

He mailed that box to me before he boarded the plane that day. I could barely keep it together.

I placed one of the copies on my bookshelf, and I still have it today. It serves as a constant reminder, not just of the prayer warrior the book is about but also of the prayer warrior who gave it to me.

### The Perfect Place to Launch Our Mission

Two years later, in 2001, when baseball was all over for me, I took a job as the ministry coordinator for the David Drye Company. It was a position Mr. Drye had created before his death with a two-fold purpose: to be a chaplain for the employees and outreach coordinator for the community.

Within two years, our entire Benham family relocated to Concord, in large part because of the doors the David Drye Company opened for us. When my brother got out of baseball the next year in 2002, he took a job as the janitor at David Drye's school. Our sister, Tracy, became the David Drye Company secretary, and our dad was part of the pro-life outreach the company supported. Even in death, David Drye's life brought divine connection for our family—helping establish the plan God had for us here on earth.

By the time 2014 rolled around and the Kendrick Brothers told us about their idea for making a movie about the power of prayer, we knew there was only one place it could be filmed— right where the embodiment of the message took his last breath. To us, *War Room* served as a tribute to the life David Drye.

There is a scene in the movie where Tony comes into a gym, sees his daughter jumping rope, and stands there as a proud daddy smiling in awe of what she can do. That scene was filmed in the gymnasium of the school David Drye founded and funded with his generous Kingdom giving. Now his investment has been seen all over the world in a movie that itself is a testament of how God answered his prayers.

One of the most powerful ways you can stand in the gap— for others, for your family, and for this nation—is through prayer. Prayer is where the real battle is fought and won. It's where boldness meets brokenness and heaven collides with earth.

Pray like David Drye prayed—on your knees with fierce faith, asking God to bust the rocks and break the chains of the enemy. Pray that your life will be a bridge God uses to connect His power to those who desperately need it. Because none of us knows when we've prayed our last prayer or lived our last day.

In the end, the strength to stand in the gap always begins when you kneel in the gap, alone with God. Boldness in private always precedes boldness in public. And if you truly want to be a bridge between heaven and earth, there is no other way.

## CHAPTER SEVENTEEN

# FLAWED AND FAITHFUL

*"God can strike a straight blow with a crooked stick."*
–Martin Luther

~~~

Quite often, after speaking engagements, men come up to us with the same confession: *"I want to stand bold for the Lord ... but my past disqualifies me."* What they don't realize—and what we've seen again and again—is that God doesn't call the flawless; He calls the faithful. He doesn't use perfect vessels; He uses broken ones. And in His hands, those cracks become the very places His glory shines through.

Unfortunately, today's cancel culture thrives on public shame. Social media doesn't let men move forward; it chains them to their past. Even after repentance, the accusations keep coming—over and over—until many believe they're permanently disqualified from serving the Lord. But that's not the gospel. That's a culture of condemnation, and it's killing the courage of men who could be powerful for God. These cancel culture critics are bent on *destruction,* not *restoration.*

But one look at Scripture and we clearly see how God redeems the faults and sinful deeds of countless men and women and uses them in powerful ways. He didn't use perfect people;

He used broken people—those marred by sin but forgiven by God. Abraham was a liar. Jacob was a deceiver. Aaron was an idolater. Rahab was a prostitute. David was an adulterer. Paul was a murderer. The list goes on. The Bible hides nothing about the men and women God used to bring heaven to earth in real ways. And the key to His use of them was not their *perfect*ness but their *broken*ness.

We love how Warren Wiersbe, one of our favorite Bible commentators, put it:

"Every great personality mentioned in the Bible sinned at one time or another. Abraham lied about his wife (Gen. 12:10–20). Moses lost his temper and disobeyed God (Num. 20:7–13). Peter denied the Lord three times (Matt. 26:69–75). But sin was not the settled practice of these men. It was an *incident* in their lives, totally contrary to their normal habits. And when they sinned, they admitted it and asked God to forgive them."

This is what the faithful believers before us did. They were broken over their sin and submitted their selfish, stubborn ways to God. If we didn't get to see their raw, real-life *incidents* of sin, we'd all probably throw our hands up in despair and wonder how, or if, God could ever use us today. But God didn't do that to us; instead, He brought us into the darkest, most intimate secrets of their lives and showed how broken people can be restored *to* Him and then used *for* Him in powerful ways.

## Owning Our "Wretchedness"

Every time we sing "Amazing Grace," we love how spot-on the third line is: "that saved a *wretch* like me." John Newton wrote the song in 1779. He was a slave trader who came to faith and repented of his sins, penning this song in the glorious days after his conversion. Some contemporary versions of the song omit this line, perhaps because this is where the rubber meets the road for many believers today. So many times, we conceal our sinfulness for fear of getting smeared by others and not being useful to God anymore.

But God destroys shame in the light of truth. When we share our true selves honestly, we bring heaven to earth like nothing else. The power of our testimony—how we were broken, restored, and then used by God—stands as hope and mercy for others.

I (David) will be the first to admit what a pathetic sinner I've been. I've lied, cheated, gossiped, stolen, and more. I've been hypocritical and judgmental. I've blessed God from one side of my mouth while cursing out the other. But I've grown in the Lord; those sinful ways are not part of my lifestyle anymore. As a young man, I had *habits* more than *incidents*, like struggles with deceit, lust, and anger. But as I've walked in God's light, the gentle heat of His presence has burned those habits away. It's kind of like feeling heat the closer you get to a light source.

As an older man, I still have incidents from time to time. We all do. Here are three I've struggled with over the years.

The biggest issue in my adult life used to be losing my temper. When my kids were younger, I was so concerned about their being perfect that any misbehavior—foolish or willful—would be met with angry correction. I didn't shepherd their hearts beside the "still water" like the Good Shepherd, but—

more like a mean shepherd—I led them to the "rushing torrent" of angry, verbal correction. Yet God broke me of this, and He used my youngest son to do it.

Our family was watching a pre-release movie with our friends the Kendricks. It's one of the fringe benefits we get for hanging out with them—they see all the newest faith-based releases before they hit theaters. There was a scene halfway through this movie where the dad totally lost it and yelled angrily at his son, looking like he wanted to hit him. When the scene ended, my youngest boy crawled onto my lap, and with his thumb in his mouth he looked at me and whispered, "Daddy, would you ever do that to me?"

I couldn't believe he asked me that question. I wondered, *Have I developed such a fear in my boy that he actually thinks I may lose it on him like this guy? What a stinkin' wretch I am!*

My heart broke. Here was my son, sitting in my lap with his thumb in his mouth, looking at me with eyes longing, even begging, for me to assure him I would never do such a thing to him. Thankfully, I never did anything like that before, but the sheer fact he asked meant I had already damaged his little heart.

I wrapped him in my arms tighter than ever, and with tears in my eyes, I promised him—from the bottom of my heart—I would never do that to him. I also begged him to forgive me for making him feel that way. God literally broke me with one simple question from my son.

I told my wife what he'd said, and over the next few days, she helped me see even more clearly what anger can do to a child's heart. I finally saw the light. I asked God to forgive me and then pulled all my kids into the living room to repent. I asked for their forgiveness and committed to fully submit to God in that area of my life. Today, I'm a broken father, fully restored and able to lead much better.

## Ambition in the Wrong Seat

Just about the time I got my anger under control, I realized I needed to do the same with my ambition. Jason and I are entrepreneurs, which means we know how to make things happen and move stuff forward. We have discovered, however, that ambition is an entrepreneur's best friend—so long as it stays in the passenger seat. The minute it jumps into the driver's seat, you'll end up going the wrong way.

I saw this up close my first few months as a real estate agent. I put together a deal on four houses that would allow me to make a good amount of money outside of closing. This meant a certain portion of money would change hands but not be disclosed to the closing attorney. At first, I didn't know it was wrong because I was new in the industry and lots of other agents did it. But after I found out, I still tried to push the deal through. We desperately needed the money, so I rationalized that it wouldn't be a big deal. Besides, if other agents did it, then it couldn't be that bad. But it was still wrong—and I knew it.

I told Jason about the deal, and he questioned me. "Are you sure we're supposed to do that?"

"We'll be fine," I told him, "Besides, there's nothing *really* wrong here because everyone involved is fully aware of what's going on."

Uh, that didn't matter—because it was wrong. Thankfully, God used my broker in charge to show me the error of my ways.

"Guys. Any time you overstate a price and try to get money outside of closing, it's illegal," he said. "You boys are going to make enough money in real estate. Just do it the right way."

I knew in my heart he was right. So, I pulled out of the deal, lost a little bit of money, and asked God to forgive me for letting my ambition take the lead. Years later, and with my conscience fully intact, my brother and I ended up building one of the fastest-growing private real estate franchises in America. Only God. I was broken of my selfish ambition and let God-honoring ambition—full of honesty—drive us to success.

## Emotions in the Wrong Seat

Although I learned to harness my ambition, I had to learn to harness my emotions as well. Early in my marriage, I made sure all the doors of my heart were locked tight (from pornography, etc.), yet one time I failed to realize a small window that was cracked open. And God used my brother to bring it up to me. I didn't believe him at first—I was blind to it—because in my mind the major doors of my heart were closed. I didn't feel the draft from this "little" window at all.

I was always friendly with girls growing up, but the truth is, I crossed the line into being a flirt—even into the early years of my marriage. I never would've admitted it then, but I can now. I thank God He's restored me and helped me build strong boundaries, but back then I didn't have the guardrails I needed. There was a time when I allowed myself to grow too close to another woman. It never became sexual, thankfully, but it still grew inappropriate and sinful. It's painful to admit, but there's freedom in honesty and vulnerability—because God's grace is greater than our failures. And when you've been forgiven, you can't help but share your testimony.

Thankfully, God won the victory and provided a way out for me—just like His Word says, "No temptation has overtaken you except what is common to mankind. And God is faithful; He will not let you be tempted beyond what you can bear. But when you are tempted, *He will also provide a way out* so that you can endure it" (1 Corinthians 10:13, emphasis added).

Jason was God's way out for me. He hit me with a hard rebuke, which awakened me to the reality of the path that I was on. I immediately stopped dead in my tracks and opened up to him, and then I told my wife and asked for forgiveness. I told my pastor, too, and other men in the church who could hold me accountable. I also went to her husband, and he graciously forgave me. I repented to God and then slammed that window shut, tight—forever.

So many years have passed since then, and to this day, there remains a security and safety with God-honoring boundaries in my life more than I could have ever imagined. I continue to grow closer to the Lord and my wife, not as a perfect man but as a broken one, fully submitted to my King.

## How God Uses Broken People

Through my own struggles, I've seen firsthand how God uses broken people (humbled over their sin) not perfect people (without sin).

Sin is a destroyer, but God is a Restorer. Maybe you've been caught in sin's grip before. Maybe you didn't have a brother (or sister) to stand in the gap for you. Or perhaps you refused to listen, ended up walking further down sin's path, and have suffered greatly. Can God still use you? Or are you just going to be left on the scrap heap of Christian history, ineffective for Him?

I have good news for you—God can and will use you if you let Him. Broken horses are useful horses. Our dad used to say, "Only the horses willing to be broken by the master are fit to pull the king's chariot. The rest are left to pasture." So, if you've confessed your sins and forsaken them, assuming full responsibility for your actions and accountability for future ones, then you are a broken person God can use in mighty ways. As a matter of fact, if you take your *mess* and give it some *age* (some time), you end up with a *message*—and often even a ministry! God is just that good.

But Satan wants you to stay trapped in fear, guilt, and shame. He doesn't want you to stand in the gap and do the will of God. He's an accuser, so whenever God wants to use you, Satan will be right there to whisper in your ear, reminding you of the "wretch" you once were (see Zechariah 3:1–5). But you have to speak the truth: God's amazing grace "saved a wretch like me."

## Baseless Accusations

Before the 2012 Democratic National Convention in Charlotte, I felt the Lord leading Jason and me to spearhead a citywide prayer service for revival and awakening the night before. That's when I heard the accusation for the first time: *"You can't be used by God,"* followed by the memory of sins in the past—sins for which I had already been forgiven.

Thankfully, God brought Psalm 66:18–19 to my mind. The man after God's own heart (David) said, "If I had cherished sin in my heart, the Lord would not have listened; but God has surely listened and has heard my prayer." So, I knew in my mind God would hear my prayers. I wasn't cherishing sin in my heart. I was fully submitted to His will and ways, but this voice kept coming back.

*"You can't be used by God."*

It was a real battle for me. I had no trouble leading in small ways, but a project of this magnitude felt more intense. Yet, as the accusations came with each passing day, the voice of the Lord in my spirit began to come even louder and more frequently.

"Gather My church for prayer."

The more I watched our nation decline spiritually and morally, the more I heard the urgency of the Lord's call. So, I spent dedicated time in prayer over it, asking God how He could use a guy like me.

Then I turned to Psalm 51 and read another prayer by David:

"Have mercy on me, O God, according to your unfailing love; according to your great compassion blot out my transgressions. Wash away all my iniquity and cleanse me from my sin ... Restore to me the joy of your salvation and grant me a willing spirit, to sustain me. *Then I will teach transgressors your ways* so that sinners will turn back to you" (Psalm 51:1–4, 7–13).

Those verses spoke directly to me. After full repentance, confession of sin, and assumption of responsibility, God could use anyone to help others turn back to Him. He could use an old, broken horse like me to pull the chariot of His presence into our city.

Standing on that incredible promise, I decided to join my brother and lead this prayer service. I was a broken man, just like King David, which is exactly the kind of person God could use to bring heaven to earth. More than 9,000 people poured into an amphitheater with more than 150 churches uniting to seek the Lord that day. It was truly a supernatural event. Years later, people still reach out to us saying how impactful that time was in their lives.

The Lord continues to work in my life, drawing me closer to Him with each passing day. My desire is to be useful for His kingdom, to be a Godly husband, father, and worker. And He grants the desire of my heart every time I submit to Him.

If you find yourself asking if God could ever use you because of your past, go back and see if there's something left to confess. If so, confess it and seek reconciliation with those affected. Let God break you; He is always faithful to forgive and restore.

But then, get ready! Because He can and will use you to connect heaven to earth for others in a powerful way.

## CHAPTER EIGHTEEN

# LOVING WELL

*"Human jealousy tears down.
God's jealousy builds up—because it
guards what is most precious."*
–A.W. Tozer

~~~

If someone hit on your spouse, how would that make you feel? Be honest—you wouldn't just shrug and say, "Well, that's flattering." No, something in you would flare up. You'd be ready to step in, maybe even "lay hands" on somebody, and not in the prayer meeting way! Why? Because that's your person, and you'd fight to protect what's yours.

If you're not married, you still get this. Think about your little sister, your best friend, or even your mom. If someone came after them, you'd feel the same thing—that protective fire rising up inside you. That's jealousy. And in the right context, it's a good thing.

We should have a jealous love for our spouse—the godly kind that protects, not the toxic kind that envies. Godly jealousy says, "This is the one God gave me, and I will guard our relationship everything I've got." Without a healthy dose of that kind of jealousy, our love may not be as deep as we think it is.

That's the kind of love God has for us. Scripture says:

*"For the Lord, whose name is Jealous, is a jealous God"* (Exodus 34:15).

His jealousy isn't petty or insecure—it's passionate. It burns to protect what belongs to Him.

Those who stand in the gap for others operate out of a spirit of love—a deep love for God and the people He created. Typically, we think this means we're supposed to feel all "ooey-gooey-mushy" about the Lord, where we want to sit on His lap while He holds our head against His chest. But that's only one aspect of love. True love also feels like a holy fire burning inside your chest as it seeks the protection and affection of the one you desire.

How often do we feel that for God? He certainly feels that for us. But what goes on in our hearts when His reputation is smeared in culture, when He is misrepresented, when He is mocked and even cursed? Do we feel a holy jealousy to protect the One we desire—to sit between Him and the gross mischaracterization of Him? How about when His kids are being persecuted for living out their faith? Are we jealous enough to stand in the gap for them, too, because we love God's family?

If I overheard someone bad-mouthing Tori or saying false things about her but I just blew it off and acted like it was no big deal, what would that communicate about my love? Or what if I sat there and said nothing in her defense because I feared what people would think of me? What kind of love is that?

It would not be love. Because love looks like something, and sometimes it looks like a good dose of righteous jealousy— one that protects and defends.

Throughout the Bible, we see the jealous love of God for us because we are the apple of His eye and the jewel of His creation. He doesn't want the devil to snatch us away from Him. He wants our affection, and He offers us His protection. But how jealous are we for Him? If we love Him, we should be. If we're going to stand in the gap, we have to be.

## Jealous for Truth

I (Jason) saw this concept of holy jealousy for God lived out by my wife, Tori, once when we were on vacation. It surprised me because she's probably the least confrontational person I've ever known. Engaging in conflict for her runs a close second to the thought of smooching me in the morning before I brush my teeth—it ain't happening.

I'll let her tell the story.

*Tori:*

We'd just arrived for our annual beach trip with my side of the family. We unpacked the car at the condo. The smell of my mom's cooking officially welcomed us to vacation, so I plopped down on the freshly made bed to scroll through Facebook. Vacation seems to welcome these types of indulgences.

"Christian artist comes out gay" blasted across my news feed several times. That was an attention grabber, for sure, but I was quickly distracted by my kids' sunscreen-plastered faces, begging me to hit the beach. So, I dropped the phone on the bed and headed out to the salty air.

After dinner, a walk on the beach, baths, and kisses goodnight, I dropped back onto the bed where my phone was waiting. This time, I saw a message from a friend right away.

"Have you seen all the articles circulating about the Christian singer leaving his wife and kids?" she asked. "He professes Jesus as Lord yet is leaving his family because he's attracted to men—and he's being hailed a hero for doing it. Our cousin is struggling with the same thing and articles like these make it tough because we love him so much, want him to embrace the freedom He has in Christ, and live in the power of that freedom. We need help."

After an hour or so of reading various articles along with the comment threads beneath, my brain hurt almost as much as my heart. It was mass confusion. The thought of my kids soon having to navigate truth through the tornado of stories and opinions such as this on social media had me wide awake. I rested my head on the headboard, staring at a starfish hanging on the wall. Then I remembered a comment from one of my favorite pastors. It echoed through my brain, "What does love require of you?"

So, I turned back to my phone. What were the Christian leaders saying on social media—the ones I respected and trusted? What did their love for God require of them at this moment, as leaders of people in a culture embracing a lie? In the whirlwind of confusion, I was craving truth communicated with compassion and clarity. But I couldn't find anything. Nobody was speaking up about this very public media story.

"It will take time," I told myself.

Vacation was coming to an end, and although our days were filled with play and togetherness by the sea, below the surface I felt the tension of that lingering question in my head, "What does love require of you?" I'd begun to see the phrase, "Love wins" repeatedly over the last few months in articles imploring me to let people love whomever they want. But what did they mean by love?

I didn't want to keep reading, and I definitely didn't want to say anything on social media. I was on vacation, after all. I'd rather ignore it all and enjoy life. That would be the easiest approach. Avoid conflict, keep the peace, and make everyone happy. That's my natural bent anyway.

But I am a parent of four kids. If I took this same approach of keeping quiet about truth to avoid conflict with my kids, I wouldn't be loving them well at all. I can't take the easy way out and avoid tough conversations. Well, the truth is I can and sometimes do. But it doesn't end well in the long term for them, that's for sure.

"What does love require me to do?"

The more I thought about it, the more I realized love doesn't win: *love has already WON!* And because love won—at the cross through the death of Jesus—we can live powerfully in that love through a transformed life in Him. We aren't the same anymore. We don't find our identity in our sinfulness or sexuality—we find our identity in Christ as we walk in victory. "That's the win people are really searching for," I thought.

"We really need help with this," I began to pray. "Lord, raise up a well-respected pastor who will bring clarity to this issue for your people.

The words, "What does love require of you?" again fell back on me.

I felt strongly that I needed to call the pastor who preached the sermon that taught me to ask this question. His name was Andy Stanley, one of the most well-known pastors in America. Jason and I attended his church in Atlanta when we first got married.

I didn't know how to communicate what I was feeling inside, so I guess you could say I was calling in the big dogs for help. I thought about how much it would help my friend with her cousin if this pastor would bring some clarity to the confusion over sexual identity.

I called the church and left a message. Within a day, a representative from the leadership team called me back. I explained the reason for my call, told her we used to attend there, and asked if Andy has ever made a public statement about marriage and sexual identity; and if he hasn't, would he consider doing it now in light of the firestorm of opinions circulating among Christians over this particular issue.

I don't do stuff like this—ever. But, I felt a fire deep in my heart that would not allow me to sit silently as the truth of

God's design for sexuality was twisted in a whirlwind of public opinion.

I told her, in a time when sexual identity is being defined by sexual liberty, it seems love requires us to communicate the truth of God that can set people free as they find their true identity in Christ.

"But the problem is," I said, "it seems the church is divided on this topic. So, I guess my question is—as your pastor once taught my husband and me—what does love require of us today? We need help communicating truth with love and compassion. Your pastor has such a gift of communicating the truths of God's word—how is he articulating this in your church?"

"Our official response," she responded with hesitation in her voice, "is that we are intentionally vague on this topic. We purposefully do not address this at our church."

*Pause.* I took a deep breath as I tried to process her response.

"If we got into this discussion," she continued, "half our congregation would leave."

"But right now," I responded, knowing I needed to press in, "the world is asking the question publicly. To avoid the truth we know sets people free seems ..." I paused for a moment, "well, not very loving."

"That's your tension," she responded. "That's just your way of making yourself feel better." She then proceeded to tell me how we tend to make issues like this more about ourselves than the person we are trying to love—I was somehow operating out of guilt, and this wasn't good.

"I really don't think so," I responded. "If it were just about me, I would let it go and get on with life. My nature is to be that person who just understands and affirms the things that make everyone feel happy. I really like to be liked. But protecting myself and my reputation over someone's well-being and soul doesn't seem to be the proper posture for Christians. It's not what love requires of me, right?"

The conversation went on for some time but progressed no further. It was "my tension," she said several times. Her voice was kind and calm as she made it very clear why this particular pastor was radio silent on this important issue.

I reached out in the hope that the pastor I so admired for all those years would actually share the only truth that sets people free, instead of letting people "guess" what that truth is. I felt a *jealousy* for the truth of God rising inside of me. I couldn't just sit silent, even though everything in me wanted to.

It made me think of Paul's words when he said, "You have many teachers but few fathers" (1 Corinthians 4:15). This pastor is my favorite teacher of all time. He's so good. But along with good teachers, we need mothers and fathers who will lovingly stand in the gap for others by applying God's truth in all areas of life, even when it could cost them something.

Everything in me wanted to stay out of it. But asking that simple question—"what does love require of me?"—wouldn't let me. I have since learned that asking this question in other areas of my life helps me overcome the natural fears that have caused me to shrink back in the past.

I ended up talking with my friend about her cousin's struggles and encouraged her to lovingly point to the freedom Jesus brings. I refused to remain "intentionally vague" about it. How could I be, when I know the truth that sets people free?

Looking back, I now realize God used that phone call—not to get this pastor to stand for truth, but to teach *me* to do it. The entire situation evoked jealousy in me to bring the love of Jesus wherever it is needed most. It may not always bring the results I am hoping for, as with that phone call, but asking the simple question "What does love require of me?" keeps me accountable to move toward things from which I am inclined to run.

Now I'll hand the baton back to Jason and let him take it from here.

## Love Looks Like Something

Jesus was always operating out of a heart of love toward people. But, it didn't look the same every time. There was a time when He was preaching to a crowd of 4,000, and He recognized everyone was hungry. The Bible says, "*He felt love*" for them, so He performed an amazing miracle and fed them all with a few loaves of bread and fish (Matthew 15:32).

Love at that moment looked like feeding people with physical food to cure the craving in their stomachs. The people loved it.

Before you assume Christ's love was only about powerful sermons or feeding the hungry, consider another moment. A wealthy young man came to Jesus, asking how he could inherit eternal life. And in that encounter, Scripture tells us, *"Jesus felt love for him"* (Mark 10:21). He felt genuine compassion for the man.

What Jesus did next rocks our paradigm of what love looks like. He told the man the one thing he didn't want to hear:

*"Sell everything and give to the poor. Then you will have treasure in heaven"* (Mark 10:21).

That's a bit harsh. Why did Jesus say this? Because He knew the only thing that would unlock this man's heart was full surrender to God—this was the key. His love for things kept him disconnected from God, so Jesus pointed out that if he wanted eternal life, it would require from him a willingness to forsake everything.

The saddest part of the story is how it ends. Check out the effect Christ's words had on this man:

*"But at these words he was saddened, and he went away grieving, for he was one who owned much property"* (Mark 10:22).

The love of Jesus broke this man's heart. Christ showed him exactly what he needed to do to connect with his Creator, but the man wasn't willing to do it. When Jesus inserted the key of surrender into his locked heart, the man pulled it back out and walked away, disconnected from the God who could have set him free.

And notice this: Jesus didn't chase him down or try to soften the message. He simply spoke the truth the man needed to hear and then let him decide how to respond. The bridge was right in front of him, but he chose not to cross it.

Love doesn't always look like what we think it should. This is why it requires both brokenness and boldness—humility and courage. These working together allows us to operate in love and possess the key to unlock the hearts of people.

## Love Is the Code

In our business, we install lockboxes on the front doors to hold the keys to the house. Without the code, you don't get the keys. And without the keys, you don't get inside. But once you have the code, you get the keys. And once you have the keys, you get inside. It's really simple.

We've seen this time and again in our lives as we seek to become a bridge connecting heaven to earth for those God brings along our path. Love is the lockbox, and truth is the key. Without love, we don't get the key, and without the key, we don't get inside.

This is why it's vital for us to walk in love—not the shallow, sentimental kind, but the true, biblical love that flows from God and sees others through His eyes. When we lead with that kind of love, the lockbox opens, the key of truth is placed in our hands, and the door into someone's heart swings wide. That's when heaven touches earth. That's when bridges are built.

Love is the code. Truth is the key. And God has called you to carry both.

## CHAPTER NINETEEN

# BE A CHOCOLATE CHIP

*"If you are indistinguishable from the world,
you have nothing to offer the world."*
–A.W. Tozer

~~~

In 2016, we released a book called *Living Among Lions: How to Thrive Like Daniel in Today's Babylon*. In it, we drew parallels between America and ancient Babylon, showing how the book of Daniel gives us a powerful picture of four young men who didn't just survive in a pagan culture—they thrived.

"They were like the chocolate chips in the cookie dough of culture," we wrote. "They mixed in, but they didn't blend in. They kept their distinct form—even when thrown into the oven."

That picture came straight from our childhood kitchen. If Mom was baking chocolate chip cookies, you could bet two little boys were flanking her like racehorses at the gate. We'd hover over her five-foot-two frame as she pulled out the flour, sugar, butter, eggs (and did we say sugar?), and mixed it all into a bowl of sweet, brown heaven. But the masterpiece wasn't complete until she added the best part—the heavenly chocolate chips.

The funny thing we noticed is that all the ingredients blended together, losing their form in the batter. We never tasted a spoonful of cookie dough and said, "Wow, the flour really shines in this batch," or, "Man, that vanilla flavoring is incredible." No—once mixed in, those ingredients disappeared.

But the chocolate chips? Not a chance. Those little morsels of goodness stayed distinct in every single bite. Even when Mom slid the tray into the fiery heat of the oven, the chips held their ground. They never lost their shape, their size, or their flavor. They stayed chips. Always.

Hungry yet? (Jason: I just caught David gnawing on his laptop cover.)

That's the picture of what it means to live boldly and faithfully in a culture like ours. Christians are meant to be the chocolate chips in the cookie dough of culture. We mix in—we live, work, and play in the middle of society—but we don't blend in. We keep our form. We remain set apart. And just like those chips are what make cookies great, our faith-filled presence should make the world around us better.

That's exactly what Daniel and his three friends did. They lived in the middle of Babylon—a godless culture that tried to blend them in—but they refused to lose their form. They stood apart, stood faithful, and stood firm. Even when they were thrown into a literal oven, they never melted into the culture. They held their shape. They held their faith.

When Daniel was thrown into the lion's den for refusing to pray to the king, and when his three friends were hurled into the fiery furnace for refusing to bow to an idol, God showed up and showed off. He shut the mouths of the lions, and Daniel walked out without a scratch. He turned down the heat of the fire, and the three came out without so much as the smell of smoke on their clothes.

Their lives became a living testimony of what it looks like to remain faithful to God in the middle of a pagan culture. And here we are, thousands of years later, still talking about them.

That's the invitation for us today: to stay distinct, to stand in the gap, and to prove to the world that even when the heat gets turned up, the goodness of God in us will never fade.

So how did they do it? How did they stay strong when their faith was under fire? In *Living Among Lions*, we share three keys to their faithfulness and how it transformed the nation in which they lived. They had:

- *Conviction* that transformed their hearts.

- *Commitments* that transformed their lifestyles.

- *Courage* that transformed their world.

## Conviction

It all started with conviction. They lived from the inside out. They knew exactly who they were, and they refused to let anyone—or anything—change that.

One of the clearest pictures of this comes not from Scripture but from cinema. Did you ever watch *The Lion King*? (We're talking about the 1994 original—by far the best.) It's a brilliant illustration of the power of knowing your true identity.

Mufasa, the lion king, ruled his vast domain with strength and wisdom. Under his authority, the kingdom thrived. The land flourished, food and water were plentiful, and life for all the animals was marked by order and abundance. The kingdom shined because the king reigned.

As with every kingdom, the son was next in line. One day Simba would rule. But the king's jealous brother, Scar, couldn't stand the thought. Fueled by envy, he plotted Mufasa's death—and when the moment came, he pinned the blame on the young cub. Convinced his father's death was his fault, Simba panicked and ran away.

With Mufasa gone and Simba in hiding, Scar seized the throne. The bright, flourishing land quickly turned dark and desolate. Vibrant colors gave way to lifeless shades of gray as evil reigned over the kingdom.

Meanwhile, Simba wandered into a strange new land and stumbled upon two unlikely companions: a warthog named Pumbaa and a meerkat named Timon. They taught him their carefree motto—"Hakuna Matata"—and raised him to ignore his past. For years, Simba lived off bugs and plants, pretending his old life never existed, blissfully ignorant of his true identity.

But as he grew into adulthood, something inside him stirred. Guilt from his past and a deep emptiness in his heart haunted him. One evening, while wrestling with those feelings, he encountered an eccentric baboon named Rafiki. To Simba's shock, this odd creature seemed to know more about him than he knew about himself. When Simba demanded answers, Rafiki revealed the truth: he was the son of a king—and his father was still alive.

Rafiki led Simba to a stream and told him to look into the water. At first, Simba saw only his own reflection. But as the water rippled, the image shifted, and the face of his father appeared. In that moment, Simba realized what he had forgotten all along: his father lived inside of him. He was the son of the king. His identity was undeniable.

That revelation changed everything. Simba knew he had to return, reclaim his place, and restore the kingdom.

This classic story is more than just a children's movie—it's a mirror for our souls. We live in a world where evil often seems to reign, while many of God's children wander through life carefree, distracted, and forgetful of who they really are. But like Simba, we must remember. We are sons and daughters of the Most High King! Our Father lives in us, and our true identity is secure in Him. It's time we embrace who we really are—and roar again.

Sometimes we all need a "baboon" in our lives to remind us of our true identity. Now, we're not exactly signing up to be compared to a smart-aleck monkey (*David: though Jason's resemblance is uncanny*), but here's the point—we want to remind believers in this great land that it's time to remember who you are. It's time to run to the roar and step back into the life Jesus intended for you all along.

## Commitment

Conviction alone is not enough. You have to wrap commitments around your conviction. These commitments are what transform your lifestyle so that your actions fall in line with your identity. You have to set good habits.

Your life will go where your habits take it.

Daniel and his three friends understood this. They wrapped their convictions in unshakable commitments—choosing purity, honesty, and excellence in everything they did. And because of their example, we can see five commitments every believer needs if we're going to be the bridge God has called us to be:

- **Commitment to the Word** – It's not enough to "read" the Bible; we must study it, meditate on it, and let it shape us if we want to thrive in Babylon.

- **Commitment to Prayer** – Staying in constant communication with God keeps us connected to our lifeline, the source of our peace and power.

- **Commitment to Fast** – Denying ourselves in the physical opens the door to receive strength in the spiritual.

- **Commitment to Write** – We have the book of Daniel because he wrote what God was doing in his life and times. Writing anchors our faith and preserves our testimony.

- **Commitment to Share** – Telling others about Christ and encouraging them with our story is one of the most powerful ways we can stand in the gap.

These commitments are not busywork. They are the habits that turn conviction into action, and action into impact. They are the beams and planks that make your life a bridge strong enough for others to walk across and meet God.

Conviction without discipline doesn't last. If you feel stirred in your heart but never build healthy habits to back it up, that conviction will fade as quickly as it came. We call this the "Youth Camp Syndrome"—when teenagers come home fired up after a spiritual high, only to slide back into old patterns a couple weeks later.

The way to break that cycle is simple: wrap commitments around your conviction. That's what gives your conviction staying power.

## Courage

Commitments are the bridge that carry conviction into courage. When you live from the inside out—secure in your identity as a son or daughter of the King—and you've built strong commitments into your daily life, you'll find the courage to stand firm when the heat gets turned up.

Courage isn't the absence of fear; it's doing what's right in the face of it.

Before Daniel and his friends ever stood tall in Babylon, there was David—the shepherd boy who dropped a giant with a single stone. While everyone else saw a giant too big to fight, David saw a giant too big to miss. And when you look at his story, you can see all three keys lived out in his life.

He knew exactly who he was—a child of the living God—and no giant on earth could compete with the power of the Almighty flowing through his life.

David's conviction ran deep, but it was backed by commitment. He sought God in prayer, he knew God's Word, and he practiced with his sling until he was deadly accurate. Taking Goliath down with one shot wasn't luck—it was the fruit of healthy habits.

And when the moment came, David stood with courage. He stepped onto the battlefield because God tapped him on the shoulder, and through his boldness the miraculous happened. His story shows us a timeless truth: boldness precedes the miraculous.

God wants to do miracles in your life. God wants to move powerfully in this world. But it will take your boldness. When you live from conviction, anchor yourself with commitments, and build holy habits into your life, you'll be ready to stand strong when your Goliath appears.

## Going All In

The stories of David and Daniel aren't just ancient tales of courage and bravery. They are a living legacy—our heritage—written to give us hope and to inspire us to live the same way today. For everyone willing to go "all in" for God, the book of Daniel was written for you. We *can* live among lions, because God is with us. All we have to do is stand. And if we fall, we fall standing, knowing He is right beside us every step of the way.

Charlie Kirk fell standing, and the torch he faithfully carried is being passed on to the next generation of Christ-bearers. Will you take up the torch? Daniel's faith marked Babylon forever, and our faith can leave the same kind of mark on our world. God has transformed us so that, through Him, we can transform the culture around us.

And here's the best part: the same One who walked in the furnace with Shadrach, Meshach, and Abednego still walks with us. The same Spirit who shut the mouths of lions for Daniel is alive in us today, empowering us to be faithful in the face of the lions of our own generation.

This is our time. This is our story.

So let's rise, let's stand, and let's live bold among the lions— staying distinct, standing firm, and never losing our flavor. Because, let's face it, the world needs more chocolate chips!

## CHAPTER TWENTY

# THE ULTIMATE CONNECTOR

*"Christ came not to show us the
way, but to be the way."*
–Oswald Chambers

❧

All throughout this book we've talked about standing in the gap—being a bridge between heaven and earth, between God and people who feel far from Him. Bridges hold things together. They connect what's been separated. Without them, there's no way across. And amazingly, God built that same principle of connection right into our very bodies. Deep inside you, at the microscopic level, there's something holding everything together—a tiny molecule called laminin.

Laminin is what scientists call a "cell adhesion molecule." Translation? It's the glue of the body. It holds cells together and anchors them to the tissue. Its arms even reach out to connect with other laminin molecules, creating a network that literally binds our bodies in place so our organs and systems don't fall apart. Without laminin, there's no connection. And without connection, there's no life.[8]

When I (Jason) first heard about laminen, I Googled it and clicked "images." When I saw the shape of laminin for myself, I jumped on top of my bed and did a happy dance right in front of my family. Not really, but that's what happened in my heart.

Laminin is in the shape of a—wait for it—CROSS!

Dancing now.

Go put your boogie shoes on and check it out for yourself.

This has to be the most divine mic-drop of all time. You can be whatever religion you want—Buddhist, Muslim, Hindu, Atheist, Christian, whatever—but every single one of us is held together by a cross-shaped molecule that points directly to Jesus.

Long before we had the technology to see cells and molecules in our bodies Paul wrote:

*"He is before all things, and in Him all things hold together"* (Colossians 1:17).

Without Jesus, everything falls apart. When Paul says, "all things" he means ALL THINGS!

This is life-changing. As you read this book, your body is being held together by a God-designed molecule so small you can't see it with your naked eye and it's in the shape of a cross— the very Cross to which God's Son was nailed for you.

The chief priests who pronounced Christ's crucifixion— laminin gave them the ability to speak the words. The centurions who nailed Jesus to the cross—laminin gave them the strength to drive the nails. The leaders who put the early Christians in the arena full of hungry lions—laminin gave them the power to pass those evil sentences.

Christ has always been there. He is our ultimate connector, in all things. Without the Cross, our body, our life, the whole world falls apart.

The next time you find yourself at odds with people because they think, behave, look, or want different things from you, consider how they, too, desperately need Jesus. And you can either stand in the *way* or stand in the *gap*. At that moment, be mindful of laminin—the tiny molecule that reveals the Cross in every one of us. And be their connection back to God.

Jesus has already done His part as the ultimate connection between heaven and earth. His work on the Cross holds us together internally—figuratively and literally. We cannot exist without Him. Each of us desperately needs what Christ did on the Cross—whether we know it and openly confess it or not. Jesus willingly stretched out His hands and allowed Himself to become that which He prayed about—a bridge connecting heaven to earth.

The only appropriate response to that kind of mind-blowing love, mercy, and grace is for us to do our part and share it with others. There's a dying world in desperate need of men and women of faith who are willing to stand in the gap for them.

## His Part, Our Part

What does standing in the gap look like? We hope that, in the pages you just read, you've been inspired by stories that demonstrate how being a bridge might play out in someone's life. From Charlie Kirk's sacrifice, to little David dropping a giant to Daniel facing down lions, from the everyday faithfulness of a mom making lunches to a believer whispering (or shouting!) prayers in a closet, the message has been the same: God is calling His people to stand in the gap. To be bridges between heaven and earth. To resist the lies of culture with courage and to reach hurting people with compassion.

This is what it means to live Bold And Broken.

Boldness without brokenness makes you a bully. You may thunder for the truth, but without humility, you crush people instead of connecting them. Brokenness without boldness makes you a bystander. You may feel compassion, but without courage, you stay silent when you should speak. But when boldness is anchored in brokenness, you become a bridge—someone God uses to carry His truth and His love into a world desperate for both.

That's not just a nice metaphor; it's our calling. Ezekiel 22:30 tells us God looked for someone to "stand in the gap on behalf of the land." That same search continues today. And here's the sobering part—if we don't stand, the gap remains. If we don't step in, the disconnect between heaven and earth grows wider.

But the good news is this: you don't have to be perfect to be that bridge. You don't need a platform, a microphone, or a crowd. What you need is a heart that beats with both courage and compassion. A willingness to step forward when it would be easier to shrink back. A resolve to tell the truth when it would be safer to stay quiet. A love that sees people not as enemies to defeat, but as souls to redeem.

This is what Jesus modeled for us. He is the ultimate bridge—the One who stood in the gap between us and God. On the cross, He brought heaven down to earth and opened a way for earth to be reconciled back to heaven. And now He calls us to follow His lead. To stand in the smaller gaps in our families, our workplaces, our neighborhoods, and our culture.

This is what Charlie Kirk did. In one of his final interviews, he was asked what he wanted to be remembered for. His answer was simple: he wanted to be known as a man who was courageous for his faith. And we believe he was. No, he wasn't perfect, but he lived it out, and he died for it. His legacy reminds us that courage anchored in Christ leaves a mark that outlives us all.

And his wife has carried that legacy forward in a way that can only be described as Bold And Broken. In the face of unthinkable grief, she chose forgiveness over bitterness, forgiving the man who assassinated her husband. That kind of strength doesn't come from human willpower—it comes from the Spirit of God. Her example is proving that the bridge Charlie built with his life didn't collapse at his death. It is still standing, and she is helping carry others across.

You might be asking, what does that even look like? Maybe it's speaking up at work when God's truth is on the line. Maybe it's showing compassion to a neighbor who mocks your faith. Maybe it's mentoring a younger believer, standing with them as they wrestle with doubt. Or maybe it's simply being faithful in the small, unseen moments—packing the lunch, saying the prayer, offering the listening ear.

This is our moment. This is our 9/10. The battle of ideas is raging, the kingdom of darkness is pressing hard, and God is still looking for men and women who will say, "Here I am. Send me."

Will you step into the gap? Will you become the bridge?

Because when you live Bold And Broken, you don't just survive the culture—you transform it. And in the end, that's what changes the world.

## ENDNOTE

Now it's your turn.

If *Bold & Broken* has stirred something in you, don't let it fade when you close this book. Let it move you to action.

Start by planting yourself in a **local church**. God never designed you to fight alone. You need a community that worships, prays, serves, and stands together. Find a body of believers who hold tightly to Scripture and aren't afraid to live it out.

Next, dive deep into **God's Word**. Study it. Meditate on it. Let it renew your mind and shape your worldview. Culture may shout its opinions, but truth still whispers through the pages of Scripture to anyone willing to listen.

Commit yourself to **prayer** and **fasting**. Those are not old, dusty disciplines—they're weapons of power. Prayer aligns your heart with God's, and fasting weakens the flesh so faith can rise.

And finally, determine now that you will **stand strong—** whatever the cost. The days ahead will demand courage. Standing for truth may cost your comfort, your reputation, or even your career. But remember, Jesus never called us to play it safe. He called us to carry a cross.

So stand firm. Stay rooted. Be bold. Be broken. And let your life stand as living proof that God's truth still has the power to transform hearts, heal homes, and awaken nations.

# MORE BOOKS BY
# THE BENHAMS

---

## WHATEVER THE COST
*Facing Your Fear, Dying To Your Dreams,*
*And Living Powerfully*

## LIVING AMONG LIONS
*How To Thrive Like Daniel In Today's Babylon*

## MIRACLE IN SHREVEPORT
*A Memoir Of Baseball, Fatherhood, And*
*The Stadium That Launched A Dream*

## BRACE FOR IMPACT
*A Biblical Blueprint For Building Wealth*
*And Breaking Strongholds*

## EXPERT OWNERSHIP
*Launching Faith-Filled Entrepreneurs Into*
*Greater Freedom And Success*

## EXPERT OWNERSHIP LISTENING
## PRAYER JOURNAL
*Get The Master's Mind On Your Life And Business*

# BOOKS BY
# JASON AND HIS WIFE, TORI

---

## BEAUTY IN BATTLE
*Winning In Marriage By Waging A War*

## MARRIAGE A TO Z
*30 Days To Relational Transformation*

## UNSHAKEABLE
*A Proven Plan To Crush Anxiety, Defeat Overwhelm,
And Conquer The Fears That Freak You Out*

---

*For more information visit:*
BenhamBrothers.com/Books

# ENDNOTES

1. Goodreads.com
2. Dr. Tony Evans, *Kingdom Agenda*
3. Dictionary.com
4. Tony Evans, *Kingdom Agenda*
5. Oswald Chambers, *My Utmost for His Highest.*
6. Pastor Craig Groeschel, *Winning The War In Your Mind*
7. Glenn R. Martin, *Prevailing Worldviews*
8. https://answersingenesis.org/biology/microbiology/laminin-and- the-cross/